Four Poets and the Emotive Imagination

Four Poets and the Emotive Imagination: Robert Bly, James Wright, Louis Simpson, and William Stafford

George S. Lensing *and* Ronald Moran

Louisiana State University Press

BATON ROUGE

Copyright © 1976 by Louisiana State University Press
All rights reserved
Manufactured in the United States of America

LIBRARY OF CONGRESS CATALOGING IN PUBLICATION DATA

Lensing, George S   1940–
    Four poets and the emotive imagination—Robert Bly,
James Wright, Louis Simpson, and William Stafford.

    Includes index.
    1.   American poetry—20th century—History and criti-
cism. I. Moran, Ronald, 1936–   joint author.
II.   Title.
PS324.L4   811'.5'409   75-5348
ISBN 0-8071-0194-X

Designer: Dwight Agner
Type Face: VIP Fairfield Medium
Typesetter: The Composing Room of Michigan, Inc., Grand Rapids
Printer: Edward Brothers, Inc., Ann Arbor, Michigan
Binder: Universal Bookbindery, Inc., San Antonio, Texas

For
Lewis P. Simpson
and
Donald E. Stanford

Contents

Preface

IN THE preparation of this study, two intentions were foremost in our minds: first, to define and discuss the origins of a significant post–World War II movement in American poetry that we call the Emotive Imagination; and secondly, to provide comprehensive discussions of the poetry of four figures whose work is exemplary of the Emotive Imagination but which also goes beyond the boundaries of this movement.

The poetry of Robert Bly, James Wright, Louis Simpson, and William Stafford represents the range of possibilities the Emotive Imagination affords. Therefore we draw from their work in our definition of the movement, fully cognizant that the poetry of Bly, Wright, Simpson, and Stafford has been accompanied by similar experiments by their contemporaries. James Dickey's poetry, for example, shares the interest in surreal fusions between subjective and objective phenomena; the similarity, however, does not extend much further than this in the case of Dickey. Poets less well known than Dickey, especially Jerome Rothenberg, Robert Kelly, William Duffy, and Duane Locke, were instrumental in promoting the ranges of this verse, both in their own poetry as well as in their selections of poems for magazines they edited. Rothenberg and Kelly's *Trobar* in the late 1950s and early 1960s was an important outlet for poets who were experimenting in what Kelly calls the "image poem": "This sharpening of focus led us to try to make *Trobar* a vehicle for Image Poetry. I certainly don't say that's the only place it can be found, or the only place it will be found, because the poetry of image is coming more and more to life in America." Other American poets whose careers have been shaped in part by the Emotive Imagination include Donald Hall, David Ignatow, Henry Taylor, Thomas McGrath, John Haines, John Knoepfle, Mark Strand, William Matthews, and Robert Morgan. The strongest proselytizer of the Emotive Imagination has been Robert Bly, whose influence, other than in his own poetry, has been manifest in two principal areas: his translations and publication of Latin American and European poets and his critical essays, both of which are extensively treated in Part I, Chapter 2.

It is our judgment that of all the poets writing in the manner of the Emotive Imagination the four we have selected are not only the most representative of the heterogeneity inherent in the movement, but they are the strongest as well. Their writing careers began about or before 1950, and they have published prolifically. All four have been acknowledged by major awards: Robert Bly, the National Book Award in 1968 for *The Light Around the Body;* James Wright, the Pulitzer Prize in 1972 for *Collected Poems;* Louis Simpson, the Pulitzer Prize in 1964 for *At the End of the Open Road;* William Stafford, the National Book Award in 1963 for *Traveling through the Dark.* Each of the chapters in Part II comes to specific terms with a poet's special merits, or demerits where they exist. We are convinced that, were we to diffuse our discussion by including other poets not as significant as the four we chose, our study would have superimposed the values of a movement for its own sake over the values of individual poets and their poems.

Our decision to concentrate on these four poets in our 1967 essay for the *Southern Review* entitled "The Emotive Imagination: A New Departure in American Poetry," an expanded version of which is Part I, Chapter 1, prompted our choice to write extended chapters on the poetry of Bly, Wright, Simpson, and Stafford. It is obvious to us that the poets—particularly Wright and Simpson in the early stages of their careers—wrote a number of poems that are not totally in the mode of the Emotive Imagination. We want to demonstrate, among other things, how these four poets have moved toward and (where relevant) away from the Emotive Imagination, and not to limit our discussion only to those poems that illustrate characteristics of the movement as we define it. Their contributions to American poetry do not rest solely on poems of the Emotive Imagination. We treat each poet as an individual, one whose integrity demands separate and careful attention to the totality of his achievement.

Finally, we take cognizance of these poets at a time when each is in mid-career; our discussions cannot be final reckonings. We do, nonetheless, acknowledge a significant body of verse, sufficient indeed for analysis and appraisal.

George S. Lensing
University of North Carolina at Chapel Hill

Ronald Moran
Clemson University

Acknowledgments

The authors gratefully acknowledge permission to quote from the works of the following authors:

ROBERT BLY

Excerpts from *Silence in the Snowy Fields,* copyright © 1962 by Robert Bly, reprinted by his permission. Fragments of poems from *The Light Around the Body,* copyright © 1967 by Robert Bly, reprinted by permission of Harper & Row, Publishers, Inc. Fragment of the poem "Water Drawn Up Into the Head" from *Sleepers Joining Hands,* copyright © 1973 by Robert Bly, reprinted by permission of Harper & Row, Publishers, Inc. "Like the New Moon I Will Live My Life" from *Jumping Out of Bed,* copyright © 1973 by Robert Bly, used by permission of Barre Publishing Company (a division of Crown Publishers, Inc.).

JAMES WRIGHT

"To the Ghost of a Kite" by James Wright, reprinted by his permission. Poems and excerpts from poems, copyright © 1957, 1958, 1960, 1961, 1962, 1963, 1967, 1968, 1969, 1971 by James Wright, reprinted from *Collected Poems* and *The Green Wall* by permission of Wesleyan University Press. Excerpts of poems,

Lines of poetry from "Meditation at Oyster River," copyright ©
1960 by Beatrice Roethke, Administratrix of the Estate of
Theodore Roethke, are from *The Collected Poems of Theodore
Roethke*. Reprinted by permission of Doubleday & Company, Inc.

Chapter 1, Part I, is a revised version of "The Emotive Imagination: A New Departure in American Poetry," which first appeared in the *Southern Review*, n.s. III (Winter, 1967), 51–67.

For a stipend awarded toward the completion of this manuscript, the authors extend special appreciation to the National
Endowment for the Humanities.

Part I The Emotive Imagination

1　A Definition

SINCE the 1950s a group of gifted American poets have created a body of verse that we call the Emotive Imagination. In combining certain techniques and themes, it is sufficiently distinct to warrant definition and analysis. Robert Bly, James Wright, Louis Simpson, and William Stafford are its central figures. Their work represents a new departure from a poetry that since World War II has often fallen into the categories of the Academic, the Beat, and the Projectivist. It is indebted to none of these directly nor to the schools which dominated American poetry between the wars, even though its emergence is discernible within the larger outlines of the tradition of American poetry.

In recent years what we call the Emotive Imagination has begun to receive a variety of critical definitions: "deep image" poetry by Jerome Rothenberg, "the subjective-image" by Stephen Stepanchev, the "image-poem" by Robert Kelly, "phenomenalism" by Duane Locke. [1] Briefly but intelligently in his introduc-

---

1. See "Jerome Rothenberg," in David Ossman, *The Sullen Art: Interviews with Modern American Poets* (New York: Corinth Books, Inc., 1963), 30; Stephen Stepanchev, *American Poetry Since 1945* (New York: Harper & Row, 1965), 175–87; "Robert Kelly," in Ossman, *The Sullen Art*, 34; and Duane Locke, "New Directions in Poetry," *dust*, I (Fall, 1964), 68–69.

tion to *Contemporary American Poetry,* Donald Hall calls attention to this direction in which he sees working a colloquial vocabulary, a simple language, and a "profound subjectivity." Hall understands that this newness is based on the way in which the imagination is used: "It reveals through images . . . general subjective life. This universal subjective corresponds to the old objective life of shared experience and knowledge." [2] Hall's comments underscore the correspondences of this poetry to the Jungian idea of the collective unconscious. As Jerome Rothenberg points out, in the new poetry "the unconscious is speaking to the unconscious. If the reader just gives this a chance, the poetry will communicate itself in the most direct terms imaginable." [3]

Kelly, in his 1960 essay "Notes on the Poetry of Deep Image," provided the first major definition of the new poetry. "The fundamental rhythm of the poem is the rhythm of the images," he declares, and not, as Charles Olson had earlier announced, the "breath period" of the Projectivist poets. The arrangement of images is therefore crucial: "The image, after its first appearance as dark sound, still lingers as resonance. . . . The subsequent image is conditioned, made to work, by the image that precedes it, and conditions, as it is finally conditioned by, the image that follows it: through the whole poem." The process of movement is not logical or rational: "Only the superior rationality of the dream is an effective impetus for the movements of the deep image." [4]

This poetry aims not so much at paraphrasable concepts as at processes of perception. Anthony Piccione emphasizes that "the 'deep image' poem emerges not as a statement *about* the mystical (or perceptual) experience, but as the process itself, the recrea-

2. Donald Hall (ed.), *Contemporary American Poetry* (Baltimore: Penguin Books, 1962), 25.
3. Ossman, *The Sullen Art,* 31.
4. Robert Kelly, "Notes on the Poetry of Deep Image," *Trobar,* II (1961), 15 and 16.

tion and transmission of an essentially non-rational glimpse at cosmic vision." [5]

The degree to which this poetry is radically new is a topic which invites debate and one here deferred to the next chapter. As a method of poetry in mid-twentieth-century American verse, however, the Emotive Imagination does appear to suggest a direction different from the dominant groupings of Anglo-American poetry that immediately precede it. The need for critical readjustment to the unique qualities of the Emotive Imagination at work is perhaps best formulated by "Postscript," the closing poem of Stafford's *West of Your City,* in which he alludes to qualities of both the Academic and Beat schools:

> You reading this page, this trial—
> shall we portion out the fault?
> You call with your eyes for fodder,
> demand bright frosting on your bread,
> want the secret handclasp of jokes,
> the nudges of innuendo.
>
> And we both like ranting, swearing,
> maybe calling of names:
> can we meet this side of anger
> somewhere in the band of mild sorrow?—
> though many of our tastes have vanished,
> and we depend on spice?—
>
> Not you, not I—but something—
> pales out in this trying for too much
> and has brought us, wrong, together.
> It is long since we've been lonely
> and my track looking for Crusoe
> could make you look up, calling, "Friday!"

Unlike the Academic poems, the poetry of the Emotive Imagination does not lend itself easily to a method of critical analysis

5. Anthony Piccione, "Robert Bly and the Deep Image" (Ph.D. dissertation, Ohio University, 1970), 31.

in which paradox, irony, and multiple layers of ambiguity are valued, at times, as ends in themselves. As both Bly and Simpson have suggested, a new critical vocabulary is necessary to accompany a discussion of the new poetry in which the reader is led to understanding through feeling rather than through charted and structured intellectuality. The basic techniques of the Emotive Imagination are timing, leaps, and muted shock—all of which work together so that the reader experiences the imaginative interplay between subject and attitude; he feels and is rewarded.

In order to draw the reader into the poem, exact timing in the use of images is a necessity. This is all the more imperative in poems of this movement since the diction is restrained (anti-rhetorical) and the rhythms are generally calm and colloquial. Many of Simpson's short poems, such as "In the Suburbs," "Birch," and "American Poetry," are timed with an uncanny sense of precision. In Stafford's "Fall Wind" timing is remarkably measured as the poem moves from "pods of summer" to "first cold wind" to "thin walls" and finally to a new knowledge of human mortality. This progression is not totally irrational, but the impact of the poem's final phrase results from a subtle yet succinct leap from image to image:

> Pods of summer crowd around the door;
> I take them in the autumn of my hands.
>
> Last night I heard the first cold wind outside;
> the wind blew soft, and yet I shiver twice:
>
> Once for thin walls, once for the sound of time.

The leap at the end of "Fall Wind" and the leaps in the poems of the movement in general are structured emotionally, not rationally. Calmly presented, the statement of shock through which the irrational leaps are made demands from the reader something similar to what Coleridge meant by "that willing suspension of disbelief for the moment." In Stafford's "Late at

Night," the speaker talks of listening to "the hailstone yelps of geese" one night. He then puts a question to the reader, after which the leap occurs and the muted shock is achieved:

> Were they lost up there in the night?
> They always knew the way, we thought.
> You looked at me across the room:—
>
> We live in a terrible season.

The instant in which the reader's recognition occurs results from an alogical process. Simpson has pointed out the mysteriousness of the phenomenon: "The elements of the image, however disparate they may be, have been brought together and fused in the depths, so that when the image comes to the surface we cannot perceive the separate elements or the manner of their joining." [6] Bly also has spoken of the direction of the poem below the level of the conscious and waking world: "I am not urging a nature poetry either, but rather a poetry that goes deep into the human being, much deeper than the ego, and at the same time is aware of many other beings." [7]

The first twelve lines of Wright's "Lying in a Hammock at William Duffy's Farm in Pine Island, Minnesota" describe in particular detail what the poet is observing, things such as a bronze butterfly, flowers, and a chicken hawk. Without a step-by-step progression, the leap occurs which both transforms the poem and exemplifies the Emotive Imagination at work: "I have wasted my life." And Bly's "Sunday in Glastonbury" employs a similar juxtaposition of images leading to a muted shock which is itself a discovery:

> It is out in the flimsy suburbs,
> Where the light seems to shine through the walls.

6. "Louis Simpson," *Review*, XXV (Spring, 1971), 36.
7. Robert Bly, "The Dead World and the Live World," *Sixties*, VIII (Spring, 1966), 6.

My black shoes stand on the floor
Like two open graves.
The curtains do not know what to hope for,
But they are obedient.
How strange to think of India!
Wealth is nothing but lack of people.

In the better poems of this movement, the reader is confronted with the unexpected, yet inevitable. And herein lies much of his pleasure. This is the case in the final lines of Simpson's "Walt Whitman at Bear Mountain":

The clouds are lifting from the high Sierras,
The Bay mists clearing.
And the angel in the gate, the flowering plum,
Dances like Italy, imagining red.

Compare this poem with Wright's "A Blessing," in which the speaker (probably Wright himself—these poets are not addicted to employing personae) and a friend cross over a barbed wire fence into a pasture, where "the eyes of those two Indian ponies / Darken with kindness." After a rapport is established between the speaker and one of the animals, "A Blessing" concludes: "Suddenly I realize / That if I stepped out of my body I would break / Into blossom." Wright communicates here by what, on the surface, appears to be unreasonable and slightly, if not completely, absurd. But his timing is perfect and the richness of the image lies in its emotional suggestions. The reader is shocked by the irrationality of the image, yet he is not offended; he is enriched, as the speaker has been, by the experience.

The excesses to which poetry of the Emotive Imagination is subject cannot be dismissed. The timing and leaps must occur with a subtlety and sureness that are not always realized. There are instances in which the leaps are difficult to justify on an emotional basis. Occasionally, the juxtaposition of images at the end

of the poem is too dissociated in the light of what precedes it, with
the subsequent result that understanding through feeling is
simply lost. Citing a particular example, Simpson himself has
noted the nature of such lapses: "This is only a series of forced
juxtapositions. Two things forced together by conscious effort do
not make an image."[8]

Apart from understanding through feeling, the poetic ends of
Bly, Wright, Simpson, and Stafford vary. Nonetheless, there is a
technical similarity which occurs with differing degrees of con-
sistency throughout their works. With Wright and Simpson, the
use of the Emotive Imagination appears with some regularity
after their first volumes; Stafford and Bly are consistent in these
uses over a longer period.

One of the most significant tendencies in this poetry is a
conscious attempt to be colloquial and matter-of-fact. Quotations
cited throughout this chapter testify to the naturalness in the
language of these four poets. Their poetry is often one of statement, not in the didactic sense, but in the direction of the
straightforward. Many of the poems begin with a location fixed
within the objective world. For this the statement method is
peculiarly effective. "I began in Ohio. / I still dream of home,"
begins Wright's "Stages on a Journey Westward"; or "We stood by
the library. It was an August night" in Stafford's "A Dedication."
Frequently accompanying the flat, impersonal statement is the
sudden outburst of impulsive and emotive exclamation: "I am
wrapped in my joyful flesh," utters Bly in "Poem in Three Parts";
and "I love the dark race of poets, / And yet there is also
happiness. / Happiness . . ." begins Simpson in "Luminous
Night."

Statement is nicely balanced by a fresh use of personifications
which are generally metaphoric. By the terms personification and
the personification method, we are not limiting ourselves to the

8. "Louis Simpson," 36.

standard handbook definition, which usually refers to the giving of human qualities to the nonhuman. Rather, in our discussion of the Emotive Imagination and its poets, we also include the attributing of all animate life, including human qualities, to the inanimate. In these personifications the reader is given a new perspective on the natural world; he is forced to bend to the movement of the poem, and he may experience slight jolts of adjustment. All of these help to prepare him emotionally for the use of imagination evidenced so frequently at the end of the poem, for making the leaps and receiving the muted shock. Wright's "Beginning" provides a fine example of this use of personifications:

> The moon drops one or two feathers into the field.
> The dark wheat listens.
> Be still.
> Now.
> There they are, the moon's young, trying
> Their wings.
> Between trees, a slender woman lifts up the lovely shadow
> Of her face, and now she steps into the air, now she is gone
> Wholly, into the air.
> I stand alone by an elder tree, I do not dare breathe
> Or move.
> I listen.
> The wheat leans back toward its own darkness,
> And I lean toward mine.

Most of Wright's personifications are drawn from the rural: "Silos creep away toward the West"; and "The wind tiptoes between poplars. / The silver maple leaves squint / Toward the ground." Similarly, Bly draws from subjects indigenous to the farm: "The corn is wandering in dark corridors"; "And hear the leaves scrape their feet on the wind"; "The soybeans are breathing on all sides." Although of the four poets Simpson seems least attracted to the personification method, his use of it is highly effective. It is, however, with Stafford that this method finds its most frequent and richest expression. Perhaps, at first, a categorical listing of some of Stafford's self-contained personifications is in order: "and a lost road went climbing the slope like a ladder"; "Pioneers, for whom history was walking through dead grass"; "the wheat fields crouched"; "The sun stalks among these peaks to sight / the lake down aisles"; "and willows do tricks to find an exact place in the wind"; and "And all night those oil well engines / went talking into the dark."

Despite the compelling similarities that exist between these four poets, each is an independent voice. Although they are colloquial, use the statement and personification methods, and, most important, actively work the Emotive Imagination, they do not employ form with exacting similitudes. For example, Stafford has a tough inner discipline, a lean, hard masculinity. Bly, on the other hand, is much looser; he does not have the "austere rhythmic control" Peter Viereck ascribes to Stafford. The poets differ as well in the subjects about which they write and in their resulting motifs and attitudes.

The power of the Emotive Imagination rests with its capacity to transform subjects of lyric simplicity into a personal and subjective instant of emotion. The result in most of these poems is a reemergence of romanticism, but a refreshing kind, different from that of the nineteenth century. Bly, Wright, Simpson, and Stafford are alike in their utter honesty of expression. These poets openly profess allegiance, not to the intellectual puzzles of verse, but to those forces that are personally experienced in emotion. It is in their *qualified* affirmations that these writers are distinguished, and herein lies the newness of their romanticism, which is, for the most part, noticeably free of the exotic, the escapist, or the allusive. There is a hardness in their poetry that breathes the agony of world war as well as the corruption of the American dream. Disenchantment with American presence in Southeastern Asia in the late 1960s and early 1970s is universal.

What they propose as a source of reliability is a resilient and tough individualism that seeks out human compassion for its only consolation.

Consider, for example, their attitudes toward their native land. These poets celebrate America with the eloquence and affection of Whitman, but not with his abandon. They have, to a large degree, rediscovered their land for American poetry; a surprising number of their poems are studded with place names of the American landscape. Of the four, Louis Simpson, a naturalized American, sees his country with the widest vision, as he declares in "Lines Written Near San Francisco": "Whitman was wrong about the People, / But right about himself. The land is within. / At the end of the open road we come to ourselves." For all his disenchantment, he has Orpheus maintain in "Orpheus in America" that "The melancholy of the possible / Unmeasures me." It is that "possible" Stafford clings to in "Bi-Focal":

> Sometimes up out of this land
> a legend begins to move.
> Is it a coming near
> of something under love?

Bly is ostensibly lyrical and much of his work exhibits a temperament of moodiness, a whimsicality spilling over into his concern about America. Bly's awareness of the American motif in recent poetry is attested by his editorship of an anthology, *Forty Poems Touching on Recent American History.* In "Driving Through Ohio," he openly affirms: "I am full of love, and love this torpid land, / Some day I will go back, and inhabit again / The sleepy ground where Harding was born." Yet, his second volume, *The Light Around the Body,* is made up of a poetry of vehement denunciation of the American government, particularly its war-making role. Bly was, in fact, joined by Wright, Simpson, and Stafford in his organization, American Writers Against the Vietnam War, in the late 1960s. Wright's early disenchantment with America is reconsidered in *Two Citizens* (1973).

The antagonism of these poets toward the representatives of capitalism, who they feel have perverted the dream America promised, is general and, at times, vindictive. Even Stafford, who has the smallest axe to grind, finds cause to lament a civilization given over to mechanization and profit seekers. He so attests in "A Visit Home": "For calculation has exploded—boom, war, oil-wells, and, God! / the slow town-men eyes and blue-serge luck." It is probably in this theme of disgust that these poets succumb most easily to excess. Simpson's "The Inner Part" concludes with a blanket condemnation of postwar America: "Priests, examining the entrails of birds, / Found the heart misplaced, and seeds / As black as death, emitting a strange odor." It remains, nevertheless, that disgust is as much a component of honesty as joy. And joy is the dominant tone of Simpson's response to America. Asked once in an interview if becoming an American had advanced his poetry, Simpson replied:

Oh, yes. It may be that the things I say about America are foolish to one who was born here, but I'm fascinated with America. There are all sorts of things that haven't been written about. That's what is so exciting to me. I would like to write a poem that would make you say, "Boy, that's the first time anyone ever described a gas station!" I was writing it, but it didn't work out; another poem worked out instead. I was talking about a filling station at night when a whole town is closed down, and I wrote: "The lights of the filling station were quivering with emotion." Now, that's what they were doing. All the other lights are out as you arrive in this strange town, and you see the white lights, the gas pump lights, quivering with emotion.[9]

These new voices in American poetry discover their kindred spirits with those Americans who are denied the ease of affluence. Wright's litany of preferences is catalogued in "On Minding One's Own Business":

9. "An Interview with Louis Simpson, Part II," *dust*, I (Winter, 1965), 17.

From prudes and muddying fools,
Kind Aphrodite, spare
All hunted criminals,
Hoboes, and whip-poor-wills,
And girls with rumpled hair,
All, all of whom might hide
Within that darkening shack.
Lovers may live, and abide,

Bly echoes: "It is good also to be poor"; and Simpson: "I have the poor man's nerve-tic, irony."

The frontier theme, long a dominant note in American literature, is picked up with renewed attention in this recent poetry. Stafford has lived in Oregon since 1948; Bly and Wright have strong midwestern roots, and, in addition, a number of Stafford's poems treat the Kansas prairie of his youth. Simpson's California poems are among his finest. In reading through this poetry, one is struck by the insistency upon an enduring American integrity, never at hand, but always westward. Stafford's "The Move to California" recalls the source of his motivation in making the move: "the angel went by in the dark, / but left a summons: Try farther west." That same angel reappears in Simpson's "In California" and at the end of his "Walt Whitman at Bear Mountain" as the "angel in the gate" at San Francisco. The frontier remains ultimately personal and human; the territory is exhausted as it reaches the Pacific. Wright's "Stages on a Journey Westward" and Simpson's "Lines Written Near San Francisco" document this. The latter poem reports: "Out there on the Pacific / There's no America but the Marines."

The use of images which seek in this poetry to unlock the reserves of the unconscious inevitably invites the use of distinct mythic patterns. This is especially the case when the poems treat the subject of the frontier or other rural and outdoor settings. By "mythic" is meant here not the poetic reformulations of classical heroic tales or documented religious parables. Rather, these patterns are the gropings for new alignments of images which will release for the reader a recognition of the unity between himself and the revelations of the natural world. These gropings frequently involve ritualistic actions often performed in a psychic state that is subjective or dreamlike.[10] The connection between some of these poems and certain Jungian analyses is discussed in later chapters. One thinks of Bly's poems set in the wintry Minnesota fields where he seeks mythic engagement with that world through snow, silence, and solitude. In the case of Wright there are attempts to break down imagistically the barriers that sever man from the world of animals. Stafford is the poet who probes most consistently for invention of mythic connections between himself and the wilderness. Asked in an interview if he "mythologize[s] his own world," he replies: "If I could think of an image for myself, instead of domesticating the world to me, I'm domesticating myself to the world. I enter that world like water or air . . . everywhere. Mythologizing, yes. I'm writing the myth of the world, not the myth of me."[11]

These poets celebrate the West with a fondness recalling that held by Robert Frost for his New England. The debt to Frost is perhaps inevitable, as Wright has acknowledged in his first volume. In Stafford also one notes the parallels—though Stafford goes beyond Frost in his use of imaginative interplays. "Something sent me out in these desert places" from "By the Snake River" is surely rooted in Frost's own "Desert Places," and Frost's theme of returning to one's sources in "Directive" is sounded in Stafford's "Watching the Jet Planes Dive": "We must go back and

10. This definition of myth corresponds closely to Northrop Frye's assertion that "the union of ritual and dream in a form of verbal communication is myth." By *ritual*, Frye means "not only a recurrent act, but an act expressive of a dialectic of desire and repugnance," while *dream* denotes "a system of cryptic allusions to the dreamer's own life, not fully understood by him." Northrop Frye, *Anatomy of Criticism* (Princeton: Princeton University Press, 1957), 106–107.

11. "An Interview with William Stafford," *Crazy Horse*, VII, 36.

find a trail on the ground / back of the forest and mountains on the slow land; / . . . We must find something forgotten by everyone alive."

The regionalism drawn upon in all these poems is never for its own sake. The focus of interest always resides within the poet's private and subjective responses. Therefore, one is not surprised at the strong influence of family in these poems (although absent in the poetry of Bly). With great simplicity, Simpson's "My Father in the Night Commanding No" reveals the complexity of his relationship with his father:

> My father in the night commanding No
> Has work to do. Smoke issues from his lips;
>   He reads in silence.
> The frogs are croaking and the streetlamps glow.

The same distance of feeling toward his father is exposed by Wright in "The Revelation" where he muses "over time and space" upon his sternness, "the damning of his eye," and then ends with reconciliation:

> And weeping in the nakedness
> Of moonlight and of agony,
> His blue eyes lost their barrenness
> And bore a blossom out to me.
> And as I ran to give it back,
> The apple branches, dripping black,
> Trembled across the lunar air
> And dropped white petals on his hair.

Of these poets it is Stafford who is most haunted by memories of his father. He can evoke the comic imagination of his father in "Mouse Night: One of Our Games," his unique eccentricity in "Parentage," or his intuitive love for nature in "Listening." But it is the firm bond of affection for his father that Stafford sings unabashedly, without fear of sophisticates or Freudians: "My father and I stood together while the storm went by."

The figures who inhabit the work of Wright are varied. The

dead rise up in his poems to impinge upon his imagination. Victims of drownings make up a repetitive cast; condemned prisoners are his heroes. Love poems appear in quantity in all his volumes; even though they do not omit the sensual, he treats these subjects with delicacy and restraint. Describing a love affair in the autumn landscape in "Eleutheria," he selects the surrounding details with the richness of the Emotive Imagination:

> And far away I heard a window close,
> A haying wagon heave and catch its wheels,
> Some water slide and stumble and be still.
> The dark began to climb the empty hill.

Bly, Wright, Simpson, and Stafford, whether describing the panorama of America or the privacy of family, relate a world vitally alive with a spirit of effervescence and the wonder of childhood. But the exaltations of these poets must be weighed by their disenchantment, and such a coexistence is an uncommon phenomenon in American romanticism. They remain a displaced generation alienated in a land they love immensely.

It is true that these poets are boldly fusing leaps of the imagination with a direct projection of emotion. Their poetry is incidental and subjective without being trivial and illusory. They have established their own romantic tradition. One comes eventually to ask what these poets, for all their novelty, have to tell us about living our lives in the second half of the twentieth century, about fronting the pressing political, social, and religious doubts that underlie that age. Although all have been outspoken in their opposition to American participation in the Indo-China war, their poetry does not embrace facile social and political formulas.

Bly's criticism has sought to demonstrate the reconciliation between the Emotive Imagination, which by nature turns the reader inward, and the subject of politics, which turns him outward to the world. That discussion is reviewed in the following chapter. On the question of religious faith, the four are not homogeneous. Bly's poetry approaches a tone of bitterness in his impatience with all religious faith. In the poem "At the Funeral of Great Aunt Mary," for example, he responds to the promise of resurrection with "Impossible. No one believes it." The acrimony of Bly gives way to a kind of frustration in Simpson insofar as the religion of churches is concerned. In "There Is" he confesses a futile search: "I seek the word. The word is not forthcoming. / O syllables of light . . . O dark cathedral. . . ." Almost as a rejoinder to this, Stafford, in "The Tillamook Burn," affirms, "You can read His word down to the rock." Stafford, of the four, is the most conventionally rooted in religious faith, though his poetry is without a sectarian or doctrinal program. "Most of the world are living by / creeds too odd, chancy, and habit-forming / to be worth arguing about by reason," he submits in "Freedom." There is, however, a religious tone in his reverential love of nature and family:

> We weren't left religion exactly (the church
> was ecumenical bricks), but a certain tall element:
> a pulse beat still in the stilled rock
> and in the buried sound along the buried mouth of the creek.

This "pulse beat" recognition of a supernatural power (the above lines are from "Tornado") is Stafford's most consistent act of religious faith. Wright's poem "The Angel" is clearly sympathetic to the crucified Christ, and he has written several poems from the point of view of Judas, always treating the betrayer of Christ with pity and sympathetic affection.

Without doubt, a strong theme in much of this poetry is a quiet and calm stoicism in the face of a country they find predestined to destruction. They hold out almost with desperation a plea for human compassion. "We want real friends or none; / what's genuine will accompany every man," says Stafford in "The Only Card I Got on My Birthday Was from an Insurance Man."

Stafford's technique frequently is to juxtapose two situations which are essentially in conflict; there is no outward moralizing, but the cleavage between the two situations becomes experienced by the reader himself as an emotional shock. "Vacation," an early poem, demonstrates Stafford's adeptness in the Emotive Imagination at a time before it was employed by the other poets considered here:

> One scene as I bow to pour her coffee:—
>
>> Three Indians in the scouring drouth
>> huddle at a grave scooped in the gravel,
>> lean to the wind as our train goes by.
>> Someone is gone.
>> There is dust on everything in Nevada.
>
> I pour the cream.

A similar note of human pathos which results from social indifference and isolation reappears in many poems of this movement. Stafford is strong in his demands for involvement in the concerns of the human: "The signals we give—yes or no, or maybe— / should be clear: the darkness around us is deep." Simpson, Wright, and Bly echo these beseechings in their individual styles. In "Frogs," Simpson, listening to the croaking of the animals, finds their sound "monstrous" but "filled with satisfaction"; "In the country I long for conversation— / Our happy croaking." The threads of human compassion are evident in many of Wright's poems in which it is clear that personal tragedies have moved him deeply, leading not to self pity, but to an outward concern for all the afflicted whom he encounters. "Mutterings over the Crib of a Deaf Child" is an example:

> He will learn pain. And, as for the bird,
> It is always darkening when that comes out.
> I will putter as though I had not heard,
> And lift him into my arms and sing
> Whether he hears my song or not.

The peace and security of human companionship is voiced by Bly, too, in "Late At Night During a Visit of Friends" when he exclaims: "The human face shines as it speaks of things / Near itself."

One of the major attributes of the Emotive Imagination is its accessibility to a widespread reading audience by means of its simplicity. This in itself is cause for rejoicing in modern American poetry. Like all serious movements in poetry, it is not content with surface judgments: "Your job is to find out what the world is trying to be," says Stafford in "Vocation." This perennial discovery is in a poetry which is to be felt as well as understood. Indeed, the whole process of the Emotive Imagination demands that comprehension be dependent upon emotion and that the "truth" of poetry go beyond the rational.

2 Origins

OF THE four poets selected for considera-
tion in this study, Robert Bly has been the loudest and the most
continuously insistent in his call for the "new poetry." He has
also made available numerous twentieth-century European and
Latin American poets as the exemplars of the new poetry through
hundreds of translations; the importance of this cannot be over-
estimated.

The association between Robert Bly and James Wright is the
strongest—whereas Bly's affiliation with Louis Simpson, acknowledged in *North of Jamaica,* the latter's autobiography,
seems less strong, and his link with William Stafford least so. It is
worth looking closely at these literary relationships, however,
before proceeding to define more specifically the origins (and
particularly the role of Bly) in the discovery and assimilation of
the new poetry.

Bly's interest in the work of Wright and Simpson is most
clearly evidenced in the pages of the magazine he has edited since
1958, *Fifties,* which at the turn of the decade became *Sixties* and
is now called *Seventies.* The first five numbers of the magazine
were co-edited with William Duffy, but since the sixth number
in 1962, Bly has edited the magazine single-handedly. Over the
years, he has commented critically on the poetry of Wright and

Simpson and published both their own poems and their translations of other poets.

Bly and Wright have collaborated on the translation of poetry since the early 1960s, and Bly has declared Wright to be "probably the best translator of poetry in the United States."[1] In 1961, the Sixties Press, located at Bly's home in Madison, Minnesota, published *Twenty Poems of Georg Trakl* with translations by Bly and Wright. A similar collaborative effort with John Knoepfle, *Twenty Poems of César Vallejo,* was published the following year. The two poets, again joined by Knoepfle, issued a volume of translations, *Neruda and Vallejo: Selected Poems* in 1971, published by the Beacon Press in Boston.[2] Bly has commented upon the method of the joint endeavor by himself and Wright as translators: "What happens most often is that one of us will find a poem, work on it, plunge into it, and then the other one will try to pick up errors. Occasionally we will tackle poems together. The matter of tone is so important . . . to catch exactly the right tone. In most translations, one of us did the major work, the other the minor touching up."[3]

Bly first began to publish Wright's own poetry in 1959 in *Fifties.* In the contributors' notes at the end of that number, the magazine trumpets Wright's conversion to "the new poetry": "James Wright decided this spring to abandon what he calls 'nineteenth century poetry,' and the poems printed here are the first he has written in his new manner."[4] The change in the poetry of Wright was perhaps not as sudden as Bly and Duffy suggest in the note. Still the commentary is interesting as a documentation of Bly's enthusiasm for and encouragement of Wright's commitment to a kind of poetry that earns his approval. The critical prodding continues in 1967, when "Crunk," the

1. Kathy Otto and Cynthia Lofsness, "An Interview with Robert Bly," *Tennessee Poetry Journal,* II (Winter, 1969), 33.
2. The Beacon Press is currently reissuing earlier Sixties Press volumes.
3. Otto and Lofsness, "An Interview with Robert Bly," 33.
4. "American Contributors," *Fifties,* II (1959), 56.

pseudonym for the essayist who is most often Bly himself, [5] issues a long appraisal in *Sixties* entitled "The Work of James Wright." His praise of Wright's poetry is founded precisely on Wright's incorporation of the method of the Emotive Imagination: "Two energies have been trying to get free in James Wright's work; the first is natural American speech, the second images." [6] At the same time there is a prescriptive call for the ego which informs his poems to be less "vague and shifting" and for the "psychic ground" to become more "firm." [7]

Louis Simpson has been less willing to identify himself as closely with Robert Bly, and this independence seems more pronounced with the poems of *Adventures of the Letter I* in 1971. As Simpson himself has put it in a letter:

About the visit to Bly's farm in the late fifties, I have been out to Bly's farm several times. I hope that the impression will not be reinforced—already current in some circles—that Bly reshaped my style in some essential manner. I am very fond of Robert, but any changes in my writing are quite consistent with the writing in my first book, THE ARRIVISTES. The fact is that I got to know Robert when we were both changing our styles and getting new ideas. I have never been attached to the Latin American surrealism, for example, that he is so fond of, and I know that Robert positively dislikes T. S. Eliot—or says that he does— and Eliot has certainly been a continuing influence on my work. My friendship with Bly has been based on a strong personal liking, on a mutual dislike of the literary establishment—by which I mean New York, Robert Lowell, et al.—and a certain affinity in liking poems that seemed deep, magical, strongly and unexpectedly imagistic. [8]

Nonetheless, as Simpson admits, his exposure to Bly and his poetics has not been incidental. His *North of Jamaica* recounts visits to Bly's farm in Minnesota where James Wright was also a

---

5. "Important critical pieces by Bly are the 'Crunk' essays in *The Sixties* (especially the piece on James Wright in #8; the essay on Gary Snyder in #6 is the only 'Crunk' article Bly didn't do)." William Matthews, "Thinking About Robert Bly," *Tennessee Poetry Journal,* II (Winter, 1969), 55.

6. Crunk, "The Work of James Wright," *Sixties,* VIII (Spring, 1966), 70.

7. *Ibid.,* 77.

8. Simpson to Ronald Moran, March 9, 1971.

guest. They shared an interest in writing poems about American Indians,[9] and Bly's conversation, Simpson admits, was influential: "Though I would never write in the manner of the Spaniards, Germans or Scandinavians Bly was publishing, my writing was sharpened by our talks. Besides, the iconoclasm was refreshing; we agreed vehemently about things we did not like."[10] Simpson clearly admires Bly's poetry; he reviewed Bly's first two volumes favorably at the time of their publication. In 1963 he extolled *Silence in the Snowy Fields* as "one of the few original and stimulating books of poetry published in recent years."[11] And with the publication of *The Light Around the Body* five years later, he acknowleged Bly as "one of the few poets in America from whom greatness can be expected."[12]

A large number of Simpson's poems have also appeared in Bly's magazine, and, as in the case of James Wright, Bly has singled out the work of Simpson for critical scrutiny in the same magazine. In fact, the first essay in the first number of *Fifties* is entitled "The Work of Louis Simpson." The same "Crunk" commends the poet of the recently published *The Arrivistes* for "experience" which seems "strangely deeper: the poems suggest hopeless moods, profound voyages into water over his head, massive disappointments and failures." But the main intent of Crunk's remarks is more proselytizing: "The forms he uses are traditional. The question then is, why use forms of a previous age, if within the poems, you continually suggest that that age has come to an end?"[13] This reproach by Crunk was repeated after the publication of Simpson's volume *A Dream of Governors* in 1959, though the reviewer's enthusiasm for Simpson's verse is in no way diminished. The essay concludes: "In the first article on

9. Louis Simpson, *North of Jamaica* (New York: Harper & Row, 1972), 241.
10. *Ibid.*, 211.
11. Louis Simpson, "Poetry Chronicle," *Hudson Review*, XVI (Spring, 1963), 139.
12. Louis Simpson, "New Books of Poems," *Harper's Magazine*, CCXXXVII (August, 1968), 75.
13. Crunk "The Work of Louis Simpson," *Fifties*, I (1958), 22.

Mr. Simpson's work, in *The Fifties* #1, I criticized Mr. Simpson for disharmony between form and content. He sometimes gives the effect of being simply lazy, and choosing any form that will do, just as people going to the Front commandeer any old car. At other times, he gives the effect of tremendous vigor and strength, pushing a subject to its limits. In his tragic feeling he is alone in his generation."[14] Simpson's translations have appeared with far less frequency in *Fifties, Sixties, Seventies* than those of James Wright; his translation of Rimbaud's "Marine" is treated later in this chapter.

Poems by William Stafford and even commentary upon them are curiously absent from the first eleven issues of Bly's magazine. He has openly admired the work of Stafford elsewhere, however, especially its isolated roots in Kansas, the state of Stafford's birth and boyhood: "That a poet as great, a poet with an imagination as resilient as Stafford's, could come out of there really bodes very well for the literary future of the United States."[15] In the same 1969 interview, Bly goes on to envision in the poetry and person of Stafford an anticipation of the future American poet: "In another fifty to sixty years we will have a much clearer idea of what a poet is, and I think it is going to have something to do with men like Stafford, who are able to live in this country with a certain gentleness."[16] Bly's admiration for Stafford is perhaps best expressed in a poem written on the occasion of the participation of the two poets in the 1971 Spring Poetry Festival at the University of Tennessee at Martin. The poem appeared in the *Tennessee Poetry Journal* under the title "Poem for William Stafford at Martin":

> Your words hurry along the water
> like the geese through the night skies
> feeling the currents of the mother beneath them,

14. Crunk, "Louis Simpson's New Book," *Sixties*, IV (Fall, 1960), 61.
15. Otto and Lofsness, "An Interview with Robert Bly," 37.
16. *Ibid.*, 42.

feeling their way along the invisible threads of the universe
laid down by woodchucks along narrow ledges . .
They have led me to many mothers and fathers—
    my own too. . . .

The poems of Stafford's *West of Your City* (1960) reveal his interest in the technique of the Emotive Imagination at a time earlier than Bly's experimentation. Stafford himself has made the point: "I have not felt influence by Bly's poems or doctrines, for a number of reasons, some of them related simply to timing: I did not know him or his work when I was spinning out poems in the late forties and early fifties, and once I converged with the group around him, in time, I was feeling much as they were in some ways, but without any sense of having derived from their background."[17]

Opposition to America's involvement in the Vietnam War was clearly another kind of rallying point for the poets of the Emotive Imagination. As we have seen, poetic engagement in the body politic is one of the imperatives of these poets. When the antiwar movement was at its zenith in the late 1960s, Bly began to organize a series of poetry readings in various colleges and universities across the United States. The poems selected for recitation in some way reflected the feelings of opposition to the war on the part of the participants. In 1966, Bly and David Ray collected a number of these poems and published them at the Sixties Press under the title *A Poetry Reading Against the Vietnam War*. At the same time, Bly and Ray also organized the American Writers Against the Vietnam War for the purpose of encouraging "writers and students to take a public stand on the war, and to encourage read-ins at all major campuses in the country."[18] Of the sixteen

    17. Stafford to George Lensing, July 15, 1972.
    18. Robert Bly and David Ray (eds.), *A Poetry Reading Against the Vietnam War* (Madison, Minn.: Sixties Press, 1967), back cover.

poet-members of this group in 1967, Bly, Simpson, Stafford, and Wright were a part. [19]

The degree to which the poetry of the Emotive Imagination represents a genuinely innovative turn in American poetry is a question which has already generated a certain amount of controversy. While Bly inveterately refers to these poems as "the new poetry," and a critic like Donald Hall speaks of a new imagination,[20] Cleanth Brooks retorts, "But how new is this new imagination?"[21] Although it is true that at a period in the history of American poetry—roughly the decade of the 1950s—Robert Bly began to call for absolute changes in the kind of poetry then being written, and a few of William Stafford's poems were pointing tentatively in similarly new directions, it would be incorrect to assert that the poetry of Bly, Wright, Simpson, and Stafford was radically and uniquely new. Its origins in earlier American poetry are more significant than Bly himself has been willing to admit, and, as Bly has rightly insisted, its precedents are abundant in twentieth-century Spanish, Latin American, French, German, and Scandinavian poetry. Simpson's remark qualifies the nature of this "newness": "As I describe it, this movement may not seem new, but actually it was, in the sense that it was continuing an experimental movement that was never fulfilled in America."[22]

In his objection to Donald Hall's commentary, Brooks protests that the juxtaposition of images within a poem without the

19. *Ibid.* The remaining twelve members of the American Writers against the Vietnam War are Robert Creeley, Lawrence Ferlinghetti, Mitchell Goodman, Donald Hall, George Hitchcock, Galway Kinnell, Denise Levertov, John Logan, Robert Lowell, Robert Peterson, David Ray, James Schevill.

20. Donald Hall (ed.), *Contemporary American Poetry* (Baltimore: Penguin Books, 1962), 24.

21. Cleanth Brooks, *Modern Poetry and the Tradition* (New York: Oxford University Press, 1965), xx.

22. Simpson, *North of Jamaica,* 213.

presence of interconnecting narrative statements is hardly new. The method whereby images coalesce in certain ways within the unconscious mind of the reader and elicit a response ("more nearly analogous to spontaneous combustion"), Brooks insists, is "as old as that of Wordsworth's 'Lucy' poems."[23] One might find, however, evidence of a similar associative use of images much earlier. Shakespeare's Sonnet 73, "That time of year thou mayst in me behold," illustrates a tight alignment of images. The sonnet's opening quatrain is renowned for this very reason:

> That time of year thou mayst in me behold
> When yellow leaves, or none, or few, do hang
> Upon those boughs which shake against the cold,
> Bare ruined choirs, where late the sweet birds sang.

The sonnet's basic metaphoric identity is one which brings together an outward representation of nature ("That time of year") with a deeply personal, interior state ("in me"). The interaction between these two states then occurs in the next three lines. Two images are juxtaposed: "yellow leaves" hanging upon "boughs which shake against the cold" and "Bare ruined choirs, where late the sweet birds sang." The relation between the two images, though syntactically apposite, is not perfectly logical—a disparity for which John Crowe Ransom faults the poem: "I refer to the two images about the boughs. It is one thing to have the boughs shaking against the cold, and in that capacity they carry very well the fact of the old rejected lover; it is another thing to represent them as ruined choirs where the birds no longer sing. The latter is a just representation of the lover too, and indeed a subtler and richer one, but the two images cannot, in logical rigor, coexist. Therefore I deprecate *shake against the cold.*"[24] At the other extreme, William Empson, in *Seven Types of Ambiguity,* ingeniously

---

23. Brooks, *Modern Poetry and the Tradition,* xx.
24. John Crowe Ransom, *The World's Body* (Port Washington, N. Y.: Kennikat Press, 1938), 297–98.

acclaims the second image and its context for a wealth of associations. [25] Empson's reading, though far too intellectually literal for
Bly's taste, is closer to the method of association promoted by him;
and while Bly would readily concur with Ransom that such a
process of poetry ineluctably contradicts "logical rigor," he would
see this in the poem's favor.

The movement in American poetry which the work of the
Emotive Imagination perhaps most clearly resembles is that of
Imagism. Beginning in London in 1908, T. E. Hulme and, later,
Ezra Pound prescribed through both written statement and direct personal encouragement a new kind of verse that self-
consciously broke off from older themes and forms. Hulme's imperative that the poem should not conform to standard metrical
patterns provided the justification for free verse, a principal tenet
of Imagism. A half-century later, Bly argued that the same battle
had to be refought: "This old style, with the iamb, its caesuras, its
rhymes, its thousands of rhythms reminding us of other poems
and other countries . . . its elegant stanzas, its old tested devices
of pauses and counterpauses, is like a man speaking who gestures
too much." [26] The two groups also share a preference for the short
poem unfreighted with rhetorical commentary and presenting
one or more images as directly and exactly as possible: "Direct
treatment of the 'thing,' whether subjective or objective," [27] according to F. S. Flint, and "that which presents an intellectual
and emotional complex in an instant of time" [28] by Pound's stan-

---

25. Empson's argument follows: "because ruined monastery choirs are places in
which to sing, because they involve sitting in a row, because they are made of wood, are
carved into knots and so forth, because they used to be surrounded by a sheltering building
crystallised out of the likeness of a forest, and coloured with stained glass and painting like
flowers and leaves, because they are now abandoned by all but the grey walls coloured like
the skies of winter, because the cold and Narcissistic charm suggested by choir-boys suits
well with Shakespeare's feeling for the object of the Sonnets." William Empson, *Seven
Types of Ambiguity* (London: Chatto and Windus, 1930), 3.
26. "The Possibility of New Poetry," *Fifties,* II (1959), 36.
27. F. S. Flint, "Imagisme," *Poetry,* I (March, 1913), 199.
28. Ezra Pound, "A Few Don'ts By An Imagiste," *Poetry,* I (March, 1913), 200.

dard. Bly is, of course, highly sympathetic with such an impulse; Crunk calls it "the greatest tradition of all modern poetry."[29] The image, Crunk continues, is the central ingredient of the poem: "Poems are imagined in which everything is said by image, and nothing by direct statement at all. The poem *is* the images, images touching all the senses, uniting the world beneath and the world above."[30] Moreover, the vision of the poet who relies heavily on images, whether in 1912 or 1962, is highly metaphoric and one which tends to employ numerous personifications. What Northrop Frye says of Pound's use of images holds equally well for the later poets: "Predication belongs to assertion and descriptive meaning, not to the literal structure of poetry."[31] The similarities between an early and famous Imagist poem by T. E. Hulme, "Autumn," and James Wright's "Beginning" are obvious in their assimilation of these attributes:

AUTUMN
A touch of cold in the Autumn night
I walked abroad,
And saw the ruddy moon lean over a hedge
Like a red-faced farmer.
I did not stop to speak, but nodded;
And round about were the wistful stars
With white faces like town children.

BEGINNING
The moon drops one or two feathers into the field.
The dark wheat listens.
. . . .
There they are, the moon's young, trying
Their wings.
Between trees, a slender woman lifts up the lovely shadow

---

29. Crunk, "The Work of Robert Creeley," *Fifties*, II (1959), 14.
30. *Ibid.*
31. Northrop Frye, *Anatomy of Criticism* (Princeton: Princeton University Press, 1957), 123.

Of her face, and now she steps into the air, now she is gone
Wholly, into the air.

. . . .

As a result of these linkings between the Imagists and the
poets of the Emotive Imagination, one might expect the latter to
look to the former as models of the poetry they champion. As far as
Robert Bly himself is to judge, however, nothing could be farther
from the truth. Bly, in fact, never overlooks an opportunity to
fault the Imagists for composing a lifeless and puerile verse, one
with which he in no way identifies himself. Why is this so? In his
1916 study of the sculptor Henri Gaudier-Brzeska, Ezra Pound
in a discussion of impressionistic art remarks upon the effect
which the poem of images seeks to evoke: " 'The one-image poem'
is a form of super-position, that is to say, it is one idea set on top of
another. . . . In a poem of this sort one is trying to record the
precise instant when a thing outward and objective transforms
itself, or darts into a thing inward and subjective."[32] It is precisely this darting inward, this discovery of the subjective, that
Bly finds lacking in the poetry of Hulme, Pound, Aldington, H.
D., and the other Imagist poets. It is also his principal charge
against other poets whom he sees as the successors to the Imagists. If the Imagist poets sought to turn the outward image into
a profoundly "emotional complex" on the part of the reader, they
failed entirely in Bly's evaluation.

In his essay on the poetry of John Logan, Crunk defines the
image: "An image, as I understand it, brings together different
thoughts by inexplicable means."[33] The statement is imprecise,
but the emphasis is on the evocative power of the image which is
itself mysterious. In any case, this image is *not* the mere objec-
tification of things. In another essay, Bly repeats this point:

32. Ezra Pound, *Gaudier-Brzeska* (London: Laidlaw & Laidlaw Ltd., 1960), 89.
33. Crunk "The Work of John Logan," *Sixties,* V (Fall, 1961), 81.

"Even the Imagists were misnamed: they did not write in images from the unconscious, as Lorca or Neruda, but in simple pictures, such as 'petals on a wet black bough' "[34] The difference between image and picture is an idea returned to in still another essay: "An image and a picture differ in that the image, being the natural speech of the imagination, cannot be drawn from or inserted back into the real world."[35] The image, then, is a kind of doorway into the unconscious; the picture is the superficial representation of the mere exterior. Whether Bly is accurate in this assessment of the Imagists, at least in such unequivocal terms, is disputable, but the whole movement toward objectifying things in poetry has been, he believes, a "wrong turning" and one from which he assiduously dissociates himself.

Bly's rejection of the Imagist poets follows consistently his repudiation of certain more recent poets and schools of poetry generally regarded as offshoots of Pound's influence. The reason for repudiation is the same: they have created a poetry of things, of pictures, rather than one of the image as Bly defines the word. Although there are qualities in his work which Bly admires, William Carlos Williams and his influence in American poetry are finally judged deleterious. Williams' preoccupation with reproducing surface images betrays, Bly contends, "a fundamental absence of spiritual life."[36] Simpson argues further that the imitators of Williams "have not read Rilke, Yeats, Jimenez. They dare not read them. They could not bear the comparison."[37] The Black Mountain poets (Robert Duncan, Denise Levertov, Louis Zukofsky, Charles Olson, etc.) merely indict themselves, says Bly, when they affirm, like Olson in his essay "Projective Verse," that "objectism is the getting rid of the lyrical interference of the

34. Robert Bly, "Some Thoughts on Lorca and René Char," *Fifties*, III (1959), 8.
35. Robert Bly, "A Wrong Turning in American Poetry," *Choice*, III (1963), 40.
36. *Ibid.*, 33.
37. Louis Simpson, "Dead Horses and Live Issues," *Nation*, CCIV (April 24, 1967), 521.

individual as ego, of the 'subject' and his soul."[38] Robert Creeley,
much of whose work Bly admires and has published, is not innocent of the smudge of objectivism. In one of the earliest numbers
of *Fifties,* Crunk berates Creeley for an unwillingness to use
genuine images: "The language suffers a kind of drought from
lack of images."[39] His final counsel to Creeley at the end of the
essay is instructional: "I think Mr. Creeley should try to deepen
his own imagination, perhaps by learning a new poetry in another
language, certainly by searching for more richness of language
and image."[40] There is evidence that Creeley's work has grown
in Bly's estimation over the years,[41] but he has gone on to chide
Denise Levertov,[42] Marianne Moore,[43] W. S. Merwin, and
Robert Lowell[44]—all for succumbing to the same weakness:
"They hesitate to consider a personal poetry apart from things."[45]

Bly's disavowal of the Imagist-Projectivist tradition of American poetry is a consistent one, but it does not dismiss the significance of the tradition upon the idiom of his own and other
like-minded poetry. Simpson himself has added a corrective note:
"An image, Pound said, is that which transforms something outward and objective into an inward, subjective feeling—isn't it
this, after all, that Bly is talking about?"[46] Although the poets of
the Emotive Imagination strive in their use of images for more
alogical connections, thus appealing more to subconscious associations, poets in the Hulme-Pound-Williams-Creeley tradition
have made possible the undiscursive poem, irregular in metrical
cadence, and structured principally upon the use of images.

38. Charles Olson, "Projective Verse," in *Selected Writings of Charles Olson* (New
York: New Directions, 1966), 24.
39. Crunk, "The Work of Robert Creeley," 13.
40. *Ibid.,* 21.
41. "Hopping," *Seventies,* I (Spring, 1972), 55–56.
42. Crunk, "The Work of Denise Levertov," *Sixties,* IX (Spring, 1967), 48–65.
43. "A Note on Antonio Machado," *Sixties,* IV (Fall, 1960), 14.
44. Crunk, "The Work of W. S. Merwin," *Sixties,* IV (Fall, 1960), 39.
45. *Ibid.*
46. "Louis Simpson," *Review,* XXV (Spring, 1971), 33.

The example of T. S. Eliot, infusing many aspects of twentieth-century Anglo-American verse, has not been without influence in the work of Bly, Wright, Simpson, and Stafford. Simpson, for example, in the letter quoted earlier, acknowledges his personal obligation to Eliot as a means of distinguishing himself from Bly, who regrets the general influence of Eliot. One might almost predict the outstanding charges laid by Bly against Eliot: the creation of an esoteric and externally allusive poetry, one which distrusts the overt display of emotion. The poet who in "Tradition and the Individual Talent" speaks of the artist's need for "continual self-sacrifice, a continual extinction of personality"[47] can hardly expect to earn the approval of Bly. Neither can one who speaks of the artistic conveyance of emotion through an "objective correlative" hope to escape his censure. Indeed, one suspects that the mere term *objective correlative,* defined by Eliot as a "formula"[48] for emotion, is the chief source of incrimination. Bly's comments eschew the possibility that any genuine emotion can survive beneath such a label. Rather, it all "suggests the desire to be scientific, to study things."[49]

The pervasive and complex effect of Eliot is not so easily shunted aside, however. The early influence of the French Symbolist poets, especially Baudelaire, Laforgue, Corbière, and Gautier, shaped Eliot's work profoundly after 1908, as did his friendship with the Imagist-in-chief Ezra Pound. Bly's endorsement of the Symbolists is discussed later in this chapter, but Eliot's stunning experimentation with images, "as if a magic lantern threw the nerves in patterns on a screen," demonstrated conclusively the possibilities of a new poetic narrative. The imagist nerves of a Bly or a Stafford are far less frayed than those of an Eliot protagonist; nonetheless, Eliot's poetry showed that im-

47. T. S. Eliot, "Tradition and the Individual Talent," in *Selected Essays* (London: Faber and Faber, 1934), 17.
48. T. S. Eliot, "Hamlet," *Ibid.,* 145.
49. Bly, "A Wrong Turning in American Poetry," 33.

ages could be juxtaposed without logical connectives and in a manner which lay bare a pronounced emotional condition.

When Eliot refers to the metaphysical poets as an example of the way in which the poet could juxtapose various and unconventional images, "amalgamating disparate experience," in order to form new wholes, he points to a reaction not unlike the one desired by Bly. Donne and Lord Herbert of Cherbury, says Eliot, are poets superior to Tennyson and Browning, not solely for their considerable intellectual resources, but by the manner in which they could "feel their thought." It is the sharp emotive content immediately informing what the mind perceives that is found lacking in the work of Tennyson. It is true that the manner in which images are distributed in the poetry of John Donne and that of, say, James Wright is in many ways profoundly dissimilar. At the same time, as Eliot notes, the metaphysical poets concocted "new wholes" out of highly heterogeneous and discordant matter: "The latter [ordinary man] falls in love, or reads Spinoza, and these two experiences have nothing to do with each other, or with the noise of the typewriter or the smell of cooking; in the mind of the poet these experiences are always forming new wholes."[50] The statement, in one sense, might well serve as a kind of manifesto for the whole surrealist revolution in poetry which was beginning in France when Eliot wrote the essay in 1921. A poem like *The Waste Land,* published the following year, demonstrates the way in which Eliot himself practiced the unified sensibility in the surrealist mode. In the first part of the poem, for example, the image of the hyacinth girl is set between verses from Wagnerian opera and this, in turn, set after "A heap of broken images" from an Old Testament waste land.

Eliot has made clear that the proper response to poetry, including his own, is not altogether one of intellectual sorting-out. He acknowledges, in fact, that poetry appeals to levels of human

---

50. T. S. Eliot, "The Metaphysical Poets," in *Selected Essays,* 287.

consciousness in no way identified with the ratiocinative. The poets of the Emotive Imagination also return again and again to this question: how do the human faculties of perception respond to a kind of poetry that is ostensibly alogical? Stafford speaks of the way in which a poem creates a "pattern" or a "resonance with other experiences"[51] in some kind of archetypal fashion, while Simpson declares that "poetry represents not unreason but the total mind, including reason and unreason."[52] Eliot's most explicit statement on this subject occurs in his essay on Matthew Arnold, where he defines the "auditory imagination": "the feeling for syllable and rhythm, penetrating far below the conscious levels of thought and feeling, invigorating every word; sinking to the most primitive and forgotten, returning to the origin and bringing something back, seeking the beginning and the end. It works through meanings, certainly, or not without meanings in the ordinary sense, and fuses the old and obliterated and the trite, the current, and the new and surprising, the most ancient and the most civilised mentality."[53] Again, in "The Music of Poetry," he reiterates that "the poet is occupied with frontiers of consciousness beyond which words fail, though meanings still exist."[54]

Any poet's exploration of archetypal patterns in the music and rhythm of poetry as well as in its images clearly adumbrates the dimension of which Eliot speaks. At the same time, the surrealist method of linking images, not through clear and logical external continuity, but rather through the appeal to subconscious associations and reverberations, is another projection of the "auditory imagination." Both of these approaches are integral to the work of

    51. Philip L. Gerber and Robert J. Gemmett (eds.), "Keeping the Lines Wet: A Conversation With William Stafford," *Prairie Schooner,* XLIV (Summer, 1970), 125.
    52. Simpson, "Dead Horses and Live Issues," 521.
    53. T. S. Eliot, "Matthew Arnold," in *The Use of Poetry* (London: Faber and Faber, 1933), 118–119.
    54. T. S. Eliot, "The Music of Poetry," in *On Poetry and Poets* (New York: Faber and Faber, 1957), 22–23.

the poets of the Emotive Imagination and for both of them there are more extensive precedents within the Anglo-American tradition than Bly is willing to acknowledge.

Theodore Roethke, teacher of James Wright at the University of Washington,[55] embarked on what he called a "quest for identity" which embraced *all* living things, including the sub-human."[56] After his volume *The Lost Son and Other Poems* in 1948 Roethke, partially influenced by the greenhouse milieu of his childhood, undertook a richly imagistic voyage toward forms of prehuman life couched in intricate vegetative and reptilian imagery: "I believe that to go forward as a spiritual man it is necessary first to go back. Any history of the psyche (or allegorical journey) is bound to be a succession of experiences, similar yet dissimilar. There is a perpetual slipping-back, then a going-forward; but there is *some* 'progress.' "[57] In phraseology remarkably similar to that of Roethke, Bly, in a 1970 interview, speaks of a similar quest in more contemporary American poetry: "American poetry is attempting for the first time since Whitman to follow the path backwards toward the womb and try to make some spiritual progress by going backwards into silence and into gentleness and into nature. In order for a man to make spiritual progress he must return first to the kind of state of quietness and spiritual nourishment which he felt in the womb."[58]

Perhaps the most purely surrealist poet in the Anglo-American tradition in this century has been Dylan Thomas; his poems are far more tightly compressed with struggling and sensuous imagery than those of Bly, Wright, Simpson, or Stafford.

55. In a 1958 letter to Wright, Roethke fondly acknowledges the younger poet as "a combination of student-younger brother—something like that." Ralph J. Mills, Jr. (ed.), *Selected Letters of Theodore Roethke* (Seattle: University of Washington Press, 1968), 220.

56. Theodore Roethke, "On 'Identity,' " in Ralph J. Mills, Jr. (ed.), *On the Poet and His Craft* (Seattle and London: University of Washington Press, 1965), 24.

57. Theodore Roethke, "Open Letter," *ibid.*, 39.

58. Roger Kingston *et al.*, "A Conversation with Robert Bly," *Harvard Advocate*, CIII (February, 1970), 8.

Most of his poems do not possess the tranquillity and self-possession of these later poets. Thomas' famous letter to Henry Treece describes the way in which images coalesce and contradict in his own surrealist method: "A poem by myself *needs* a host of images, because its centre is a host of images. I make one image—though 'make' is not the word; I let, perhaps, an image be 'made' emotionally in me and then apply to it what intellectual and critical forces I possess—let it breed another, let that image contradict the first, make, of the third images bred out of the other two together, a fourth contradictory image, and let them all, within my imposed formal limits, conflict."[59]

Wallace Stevens, though certainly not a surrealist himself, comments on the vitality of that mode of poetry in an essay called "The Irrational Element in Poetry." The surrealists exhibit "the dynamic influence of the irrational." Their form, however, is so extreme, he believes, that they tend to "make other forms seem obsolete." Prophetically, he goes on to declare that their influence, while not unsalutary, will be modified: "They, in time, will be absorbed, with the result that what is now so concentrated, so inconsequential in the restrictions of a technique, so provincial, will give and take and become part of the process of give and take of which the growth of poetry consists."[60] If Stevens' 1936 analysis is accurate, one might legitimately ask if his prediction has not been realized, at least partially, in the modified surrealism of the poets of the Emotive Imagination and especially in their appeal to the unconscious through the situation of images within a poem.

The nature of literary "influence" inevitably remains an open question; we have preferred to speak of it rather as "precedent" than "influence." Even so, the workings of a literary past upon

59. Henry Treece, *Dylan Thomas, Dog Among the Fairies* (London: L. Drummond, 1949), 37.

60. Wallace Stevens, "The Irrational Element in Poetry," in Samuel French Morse (ed.), *Opus Posthumous* (New York: Alfred A. Knopf, 1957), 228.

the poets of the present always defy tidy analyses; the degree of influence necessarily remains inconclusive. It does appear noteworthy, however, that the essential method of the poems of the Emotive Imagination is not radically new in American poetry. Indeed, one could go on to speak of the profound influence of a poet like Walt Whitman on the work of Louis Simpson or, in the case of William Stafford, the value of Robert Frost's lyrics, or, with James Wright, the influence of Edwin Arlington Robinson.[61] We have dwelt particularly on the Anglo-American precedent, not only because it is most near to the particular poets under consideration, but because Robert Bly has repeatedly pressed his denial of the authenticity of that tradition: "We had in America thirty years ago on the one hand the ascetic poetry of the academic poets, and on the other hand the ascetic poetry of Pound and Eliot; and this has come down to us in the ascetic poetry of today, much of it noble."[62] The deposit of Anglo-American poetry which Bly and his fellow poets inherit in the second half of the twentieth century is richer than he supposes. Both in the Imagist-Projectivist tradition as well as in the more surrealistic stream from Eliot and Thomas through Roethke and Hart Crane, one can discern the traces of the Emotive Imagination.

Bly's denigration of the American tradition, one suspects, is not altogether disinterested. If the Americans have emphasized the objective at the expense of the spiritual, there remain other far more satisfying examples for the modern poet. The Latin American and European poets—Pablo Neruda, César Vallejo, Juan Ramón Jiménez, Garcia Lorca, the French Symbolists, René Char, Olaf Bull, Gunnar Ekelöf, Thomas Tranströmer, Ranier Marie Rilke, Georg Trakl, Gottfried Benn, Theodor Storm, and many others—have created an invaluable collection of verse. In one sense, Bly has made it his personal mission to

---

61. See Part II, Chapters 3, 4, and 2 respectively.
62. Bly, "Some Thoughts on Lorca and René Char," 9.

advertise their achievement as one from which American poets can draw. Keenly sensitive to the unconscious and highly personal resources of poetry and drawing deeply upon images, these poets offer much to instruct the Americans, Bly asserts. To provide this instruction, he began publication of *Fifties, Sixties, Seventies* and, frequently, collaborating with Wright, to translate many of these poets and publish them in his magazine.

Bly has expounded upon the method he employs in the translation of poetry—the third in the series he outlines here:

> There are several kinds of translation . . . the sort in which the guy just goes flat-footedly through the poem and literally translates it word by word can kill translation, and that is what happened in the United States. . . . Then there is another method of translation in which the person really rewrites and revises the whole thing. . . . Robert Lowell also did that in his book called *Imitations,* and he defended himself by calling it that because it was not a translation. In the third kind of translation, which is difficult, you try to be as accurate as you can and yet catch by care in language the emotional tone of the original man. It becomes a matter of how well you can use words and rhythm in English . . . so that whatever tone you are using depends on the emotion that you are trying to make blossom in the poem. [63]

As a result of Bly's work as poet-translator-editor, the poetry of these non-English, non-American poets has undoubtedly become, certainly not the only influence, but the principal one upon the emergence of the Emotive Imagination in this country. It is also here, more than in his own poetry and critical essays, that the importance of Bly to the newer directions of American poetry is greatest. Consequently, the manner by which the most highly acclaimed of these Latin American and European poets have imposed their own example through the filter of Bly warrants consideration.

63. Otto and Lofsness, "An Interview with Robert Bly," 32. Bly's own translations have not been exempt from attack. Donald Walsh, himself a translator of Neruda, berates Bly's renderings of Neruda on the grounds of an "ignorance of Spanish" and "a tin ear." "Donald D. Walsh Replies to Robert Bly," *American Poetry Review* (August/September, 1973), 55.

Pablo Neruda, the 1971 winner of the Nobel Prize for literature, may well be the single most influential non-American poet on both the poetry and poetics of Bly. Bly first discovered the Chilean poet, at least in a serious way, during his 1955 Fulbright year in Norway where, as Bly has described it, he found the work of Neruda in the Oslo library. The impact of this initial reading must have been prodigious; Bly admits that "I taught myself Spanish in order to read men like Neruda in the original language."[64] He began to translate the poetry almost at once. Later, he had the occasion to meet Neruda, hear him read his poetry, and interview him when the Chilean visited the United States in 1966.[65] Bly's translations of Neruda, some done in collaboration with James Wright, appeared in various issues of *Sixties* and *Seventies. Twenty Poems of Pablo Neruda* was issued by the Sixties Press in 1967, and *Neruda and Vallejo: Selected Poems,* with renderings of Neruda's poems spanning his entire career, appeared in 1971.

The strong appeal of Neruda's work to Bly is not difficult to fathom. Poems by Neruda incorporating the method of the Emotive Imagination can be traced back to 1924 (Neruda was born in 1904); and, in his introduction to recent Neruda translations, Bly has asserted that "the fifty-six poems in *Residencia I* and *II* were written over a period of ten years—roughly from the time Neruda was twenty-one until he was thirty-one, and they are the greatest surrealist poems yet written in a Western language."[66] Bly has been equally intrigued by Neruda's long career of political activism and the investment of political themes into his poetry. Neruda, living in Spain at the outbreak of the civil war in that country, immediately spoke out against Franco and vigorously worked against the eventual imposition of the dictator's regime in

64. Otto and Lofsness, "An Interview with Robert Bly," 31.
65. See "The Lamb and the Pinecomb," in Robert Bly (ed.), *Neruda and Vallejo, Selected Poems* (Boston: Beacon Press, 1971), 156–64.
66. Robert Bly, "Refusing To Be Theocritus," *ibid.,* 3.

Spain. In the late 1940s and early 1950s, back in Chile, Neruda himself became a political exile during the administration of González Videla, and, as Bly has described it, "miners and working people, to save his life, passed him from one house to another at night, first in Chile, later in other South American countries." [67]

Bly's high estimation of Neruda's work has been consistent for almost two decades, and he has undoubtedly contributed to the increasing seriousness with which the Nobel prize laureate has been taken by Americans in recent years. Moreover, it is perhaps not unreasonable to suggest that Neruda's poems and Bly's translations of them have influenced Bly's own poetry, as well as that of his contemporaries. Louis Simpson's ironic poem "Keeping Abreast, Or Homage to Pablo Neruda Perhaps," which appeared in *Sixties,* No. 6, and is reprinted in *North of Jamaica,* acknowledges his own struggle as a poet confronting the portentous example of Neruda. Neruda's poem, "Nothing But Death," for example, has been recommended by Bly for the easy leaps among the disparate images: "Neruda leaps from death to the whiteness of flour, then to notary publics." [68] Yet the poem is characteristic of the Emotive Imagination in still other ways. Bly's translation of the first stanza indicates the typical setting of darkness, silence, and solitude as the poem's speaker turns inward upon himself:

> There are cemeteries that are lonely,
> graves full of bones that do not make a sound,
> the heart moving through a tunnel,
> in its darkness, darkness, darkness,
> like a shipwreck we die going into ourselves,
> as though we were drowning inside our hearts,
> as though we lived falling out of the skin into the soul.

67. *Ibid.,* 10.
68. Robert Bly, "Looking for Dragon Smoke," *Seventies,* I (Spring, 1972), 6.

Although Bly's *Silence in the Snowy Fields* antedates the appearance of his translation of this poem by several years, the affinities between "Nothing But Death" and a poem like "Awakening" are unmistakable. In both poems, intimations of death emerge through images of darkness. Furthermore, the personal and psychic darkness is attained by intense introspection on the part of the poets: "the heart moving through a tunnel / in it darkness, darkness, darkness" in Neruda's poem, and "We have come, a tunnel softly hurtling into darkness" in Bly's. Bly defines in this case the elusive hints of death through the same kind of associative linking of unexpected and unlike images found in many of his other poems:

> Lincoln's statue, and the traffic. From the long past
> Into the long present
> A bird, forgotten in these pressures, warbling,
> As the great wheel turns around, grinding
> The living in water.
> Washing, continual washing, in water now stained
> With blossoms and rotting logs,
> Cries, half-muffled, from beneath the earth, the living
>   awakened at last like the dead.

There are obvious differences between the two writers, and to suggest that Bly as poet has learned from Neruda does not imply servile imitation. The "snowy fields" of Bly's verse are far removed from Neruda's Chilean settings. In addition, Neruda's poems are more surrealistically crowded with images than Bly's (many of Neruda's poems are simply longer), and the South American's poems are less frequently peopled with only a single speaker. Unlike Bly, Neruda's poems are as often urban as rural in setting. But the same associative use of images occurs through the work of both poets and the same kind of impulsive outburst of emotive self-definition: "*Qué alegre eres, Miguel, qué alegres somos!*" asserts Neruda in "Letter to Miguel Otero Silva in

Caracas." And Bly, with a similarly spontaneous avowal: "I have awakened at Missoula, Montana, utterly happy." Similar lyric exclamations occur in the poetry of Wright and Simpson.

The political poems of Bly may also reflect the example of Neruda, though the specific political controversies are obviously of two worlds.[69] Both poets protest the illegitimate usurpation of power and its misapplication by governments. In "The United Fruit Co." Neruda speaks of the "dictatorship of flies" and goes on to identify "Trujillo flies, Tacho flies," and others. Bly surrealistically presents the deliberations of Johnson's cabinet meetings, also through the perspective of insects in "Johnson's Cabinet Watched by Ants." Bly has referred specifically to "The United Fruit Co." as illustrative of the general fact that the poems of the Emotive Imagination need not deny in their content the presence of the outer world: "The conventionally wise assure us that to a surrealist the outer world has no reality—only his inner flow of images is real. Neruda's work demolishes this banality. Neruda's poetry is deeply surrealist and yet entities of the outer world like the United Fruit Co. have greater force in his poems than in those of any strictly 'outward' poet alive."[70]

Bly's admiration of the Spanish-speaking poets of the twentieth century has not been limited to Pablo Neruda. Spanish as well as other Latin American poets have also been singled out for commendation—especially César Vallejo, Antonio Machado, Blas De Otero, and Miguel Hernández. The example of Garcia Lorca, in fact, may even approach Neruda as an influence on Bly,[71] while the penchant of Bly and Wright for the elongated, conversational titles of many of their poems may owe something to

69. It should be noted, however, that Bly shares Neruda's outrage at the economic exploitation of Latin American countries by certain American conglomerate industries. Compare, for example, Neruda's "The United Fruit Co." and Bly's "Sleet Storm on the Merritt Parkway."

70. Robert Bly, "The Surprise of Neruda," *Sixties,* VII (Winter, 1964), 19.

71. See Bly, "Some Thoughts on Lorca and René Char."

the example of Juan Ramón Jiménez: "There is an interesting poem from that time [ca. 1916] called something like: 'In a room on Washington Square, with my bags all packed, I wait to leave.'"[72] Bly also commends Jiménez' sense of isolation from "politics or religious doctrine": "We can understand the subject matter of Jiménez' poems if we understand that it is in solitude a man's emotions become very clear to him."[73] The Beacon Press issued more than sixty-five of Bly's translations, *Lorca and Jiménez: Selected Poems,* in 1973.

Part of the fluidity of the poems of the Emotive Imagination can be attributed to their use of repetitions of lines and phrases. In "Counting Small-Boned Bodies" Bly begins each of the poem's three tercets with "If we could only make the bodies smaller" as a way of establishing a mounting irony within the poem. This method of repetition is peculiarly prominent in the work of the Peruvian poet César Vallejo. Scarcely a poem in the collection of translations by Bly, Wright, and Knoepfle is without repetition of lines or phrases—either for ironic effect or lyric intensity. Perhaps for all these reasons, Bly has attributed a certain preeminence to these poets: "The Spanish poets of this century—much greater than the French in my opinion—loved the new paths of association even more than the French."[74]

Although Bly seems to prefer the Spanish to the French poets—especially for the emotive content of the images of the unconscious[75]—he in no way minimizes the value of the French example. Especially have the French been significant historical-

72. "Juan Ramón Jiménez," *Fifties,* II (1959), 55.

73. Robert Bly, "Juan Ramón Jiménez Under the Water," *Lorca and Jiménez, Selected Poems* (Boston: Beacon Press, 1973), 2.

74. Robert Bly, "Spanish Leaping," *Seventies,* I (Spring, 1972), 17–18.

75. "French surrealism and Spanish surrealism both contain wonderful leaps, but whereas French surrealism often longs for the leaps *without* any specific emotion—many believe that the unconscious does not *have* emotions—the Spanish poets believe that it does." Robert Bly, "Wild Associations," *Seventies,* I (Spring, 1972), 30.

ly, Bly argues; in more than one place he has pointed to the poetry of Baudelaire and the other nineteenth-century Symbolist poets as pioneers in the poetry of associative images.

The 1961 issue of *Sixties,* No. 5, is singularly useful as an illustration of the importance of the Symbolists to the poets of the Emotive Imagination. Bly, Wright, and Simpson all have translations of Symbolist poems in this number. Bly's translation of the famous Baudelaire manifesto-poem *"Correspondances"* (which Bly translates as "Intimate Associations") shows the degree to which Bly applies his personal priorities to the earlier French poets. The poem by Baudelaire begins:

> La nature est un temple où de vivants piliers
> Laissent parfois sortir de confuses paroles;
> L'homme y passe à travers des forêts de symboles
> Qui l'observent avec des regards familiers.

Bly's rendering of the stanza betrays his own peculiar interest in the Symbolist method:

> The natural world is a spiritual house, where the
>   pillars, which are alive,
> Let slip at times some strangely garbled words;
> Man walks there through forests of physical things
>   that are also spiritual things,
> Which watch him with affectionate looks.

What is remarkable here is the way in which the translation capitalizes on the relation between the natural and human worlds, not so much as "correspondences," but as "intimate associations." Consequently, *"forêts de symboles"* of line three becomes, not "symbolic forests," but "forests of physical things that are also spiritual things." Later, in line six, Bly's choice for *"ténébreuses et profonde unité"* in the description of the *"longs échos"* is "a deep and profound association / A merging." What the translation of Bly insists upon is the correspondence between men and objects as "associations," "merging," between the outer world and the interior, psychic world. The translation is clearly not a distortion of the lines by Baudelaire, but it does pull the poem in the direction of Bly's own preferences. The perception of correspondences between inner and outer worlds constitutes the vitality of the best poets, as Bly has described in another context: "The poet . . . knows his feelings are holy and he considers the created world holy also, because he notices correspondences between its events and certain sacred inner events. Moreover, he realizes that his feelings are not only his."[76]

Louis Simpson's translation of Rimbaud's *"Marine"* is also noteworthy, not only because Simpson has translated far fewer of the European and Latin American poets than Bly and Wright, but also because it illustrates Bly's own observation about Rimbaud: that "he grasped the deep interior life flowing beneath the reason."[77]

> The chariots of silver and copper—
> The prows of steel and silver—
> Beat the foam—
> Tear at the roots of brambles.
> The offshore currents,
> And the huge paths of the ebbing tide,
> Circle toward the east,
> Toward the pillars of the forest—
> Toward the timbers of the pier,
> Where it is bending wounded with whirlpools of light.

Simpson's translation points to the major association between the Symbolists and the poets of the Emotive Imagination. The world is seen in profusely metaphoric and evocative terms by the bringing together of images that may belong to no rationally discernible pattern. The Symbolists have proved in this respect to be able instructors, not only to Simpson, Bly, and Wright, but also to

76. Robert Bly, "American Poetry: On the Way to the Hermetic," *Books Abroad,* 46 (Winter, 1972), 21.
77. Robert Bly, "Some Notes On French Poetry," *Sixties,* V (Fall, 1961), 66.

Pound, Eliot, Williams, and Stevens—especially in showing the peculiarly evocative power of verbal objects. One notes also the popular use of personifications by the poets of the Emotive Imagination—present here as the tide is "wounded with whirlpools of light."

Marcel Raymond, in his *From Baudelaire to Surrealism,* remarks that a principal contribution of Baudelaire and the other Symbolists to the later surrealist poets, especially André Breton and his followers of the 1920s, was precisely their ability to probe the unconscious through the instrument of the image:

But with Baudelaire, "the first of the seers" as Rimbaud called him, the imagination became aware of its demiurgic function. Grafted on a mystical sense of "universal correspondence," it anticipates its immense task of revealing by means of images the essential kinship of all things, the participation of all things and souls in an all-pervasive mind, in the "dark and profound unity" of the whole. Most of Baudelaire's successors were not inclined to accept this metaphysics, but if we confine ourselves to an analysis of the use of imagery for the last seventy-five years, we must admit that the surrealist catachreses represent the terminal point of a perfectly clear line of development, the various stages of which are easily distinguished."[78]

Among the later twentieth-century French poets, Bly's own preference seems reserved for René Char, whom he sees coming from the Symbolist tradition by way of the surrealists of the twenties.[79] He has published, however, poems by Paul Éluard, Jules Supervielle, Henri Michaux, Yves Bonnefoy, and others.

Bly's interest in twentieth-century Scandinavian poets un-

---

78. Marcel Raymond, *From Baudelaire to Surrealism* (London: Methuen and Co., Ltd., 1950), 261.

79. "Char did not suddenly appear from the snow, and was not miraculously forged by the accident of war, as many suggest, but he wrote surrealist poetry for years before he wrote the poetry for which he is now famous. If you look at a bibliography, you will see that most of his early poems were published by 'Editions Surrealiste,' and that once, at least, he shared a book with André Breton and Paul Eluard. This to me has enormous significance." Bly, "Some Thoughts on Lorca and René Char," 8.

doubtedly gained its impetus from the year he spent in Norway in 1955. The purpose of his Fulbright grant for the year, he tells us, was to "translate Norwegian poetry into English." He rapidly learned the language and enlarged his interest to the neighboring languages: "Swedish and Danish were very easy for me after that."[80] In 1967 he published a volume of poems by the Swedish poet Gunnar Ekelöf entitled *Late Arrival on Earth*. The translation was done in collaboration with Christina Paulston, and it was reissued with a few additional poems the following year under the title *I Do Best Alone at Night*. Translations of Swedish, Danish, and Norwegian poets by Bly have appeared throughout *Fifties* and *Sixties,* frequently accompanied by critical commentary.

Of the more modern Norwegian poets, Bly acknowledges his preference for Olaf Bull and Rolf Jacobsen.[81] What is particularly prominent in the poems of Olaf Bull, Bly declares, is the sense of suffering "without grimacing." The poems recommend themselves for their very absence of self-pity and guilt. Significantly, this sense of suffering is paralleled in contemporary American poetry, in Bly's estimation, only in the work of David Ignatow and James Wright. The "confessional" poets Bly dismisses for their excessive self-indulgence: "[They] invent more cruel relatives than they have."[82] The similarity with Wright might equally well extend to Bly's own poetry. One notes certain likenesses between many poems in *Silence in the Snowy Fields* and Bull's "Snowfall":

> What does it mean to snow?
> . . . .
> Because our old earth is sick
> of being glad,

---

80. Otto and Lofsness, "An Interview with Robert Bly," 31.
81. "Notes on Five Norwegian Poets," *Sixties,* X (Summer, 1968), 54.
82. "A Note on Olaf Bull," *Sixties,* X (Summer, 1968), 38.

> and wants to wait
> a while, disguised.
>
> This lovely snowfall
> is its deep rest,
> strengthening it to its calling,
> when it again must smile.

Gunnar Ekelöf, the Swedish poet, who, Bly notes, reached out early in his career to the French surrealist poetry of the late 1920s,[83] has been extensively translated by Bly. Perhaps of all the Scandinavian poets, Ekelöf is closest to the idiom of the Emotive Imagination, and Bly's familiarity with his work dates back to his own origins as a poet. Translations of Ekelöf's poems appeared in the first issue of *Fifties* in 1958. Unlike the Latin American poets, for example, Scandinavians like Ekelöf share with Bly in their poetry the setting of winter with its flowing images playing upon the consciousness of the speaker. Ekelöf's "The Moon" declares its images in this dreamlike fashion. The poem concludes:

> Lonesome among the sleepers,
> Backs turned to the fire, I open the door quietly,
> Walk around the corner in the snow, tramp on the clumps, see
> Moonlight coldly calling me over the snow.

Bly's "After Working," with its rich images of enveloping moonlight, concludes with a tableau reminiscent of Ekelöf:

> We know the road; as the moonlight
> Lifts everything, so in a night like this
> The road goes on ahead, it is all clear.

Ekelöf's poems are dense with personifications of nature and even man-made objects. Scarcely a poem in *Late Arrival on Earth* is without them. In addition, Ekelöf's verse occasionally points to

---

83. Robert Bly, "Ekelöf's 'Flavor of the Infinite,'" in *Late Arrival on Earth*, trans. Bly (London: Rapp and Carroll, 1967), 7.

an archetypal return to sources of prenatal life or earlier prehuman forms of existence. He yearns, for example, for such a retrogression in "A July Night":

> Give me back my world
> my prenatal world!
> My world is a dark one
> but I will go home in the darkness
> through the grass, under the woods.

Many of the poems of the Emotive Imagination describe similar mythopoeic experiences. Bly's "Return to Solitude," for example, portrays a comparable nostalgia for earlier forms of life by means of a similar passage through images of the natural world and under the cover of darkness:

> We want to go back, to return to the sea,
> The sea of solitary corridors,
> And halls of wild nights,
> Explosions of grief.

Bly's publication of the Scandinavian poets extends beyond Olaf Bull and Gunnar Ekelöf. The Danish poet Tom Kristensen and the Norwegians Rolf Jacobsen, Paal Brekke, Gunnar Reiss-Andersen, Emil Boyson, Claes Gill, Peter Holm, and even Henrik Ibsen have also been published in translation in various numbers of Bly's magazine. A volume consisting of twenty poems of the Swedish poet Tomas Tranströmer, translated by Bly, appeared in 1970, and *Night Vision*, consisting of additional translations of Tranströmer as well as revisions of the poems in the earlier volume, was issued two years later. Bly's translations of Tranströmer and Ekelöff, along with new translations of poems by the 1974 Nobel Prize laureate Harry Martinson, also a Swede, appeared in 1975 in the Beacon Press series under the title *Friends, You Drank Some Darkness*. One Tranströmer poem, "Nocturne," begins with metamorphic images similar to Bly's own:

> I drive through a village at night, the houses step out
> into the headlights—they are awake now, they want a drink.
> Houses, barns, nameposts, deserted trailers—now
> they take on life. Human beings sleep.

Tranströmer's use of active personifications, as well as the solitary setting of the poet at a late hour, induces the vitality of the dream world which is subjective but fed by the real things which surround him in the ordinary world.

The translation of Rainer Maria Rilke's *"Fortschrift"* by Bly suggests another keen proximity—this time with the German example:

PROGRESS

> My deep life is flowing on with a heavier sound again,
> as though it were pouring between wider shores now.
> I see my own nature more and more in things,
> and my eyes hang more and more on images.
> I feel closer to what no one has a name for:
> with my senses, as with birds, I climb
> into the windy heaven, out of the oak,
> and in the days of ponds, broken from the sky,
> my feeling sinks, as if standing on fishes.

Here, almost as a kind of touchstone poem, one sees the ingredients of the Emotive Imagination quietly at work a half-century before Bly began to publish poetry. Here, too, Bly finds no need to depart from quite literal translation in order to employ the vocabulary he often echoes elsewhere. The "flowing" of "my deep life" is precisely Rilke's *rauscht mein tiefes Leben,* just as "things" (*"Dinge"*) and "images" (*"Bilder"*) become the mirrors of the poet's moment of self-knowledge. Images, indeed, suffuse the poem with surrealistic linkings throughout nature: shores, birds, heaven, oak, ponds, sky, fishes. Similarly, the verbs of the poem are characterized by fluidity and gentle motion—flowing, pouring, climb, sinks—a process appropriate to the movement between interior and exterior associations. There is also a sense of an emerging consciousness for which conventional description is unequipped: "I feel closer to what no one has a name for." Rilke's succinct, declarative statements within the limits of the short poem are a fundamental element of his verse. Finally, the poem concludes with the union through simile of "feeling" and "standing on fishes."

Rilke's poem suggests the powerful resources of twentieth-century German poetry to Bly and Wright—resources which seem second only to the Spanish and Latin American poets in their attractiveness—especially, it would appear, to Wright.

Twenty Poems of Georg Trakl was one of the earliest publications of the Sixties Press. Translated by Bly and Wright, the poems appeared in 1961; five translations of Trakl by Wright were included in his 1971 *Collected Poems*. Wright has described the sharp impression of his unexpected discovery of Trakl while a student in Austria:

In the autumn of 1952, I wandered into the wrong classroom at the University of Vienna. . . . He [Professor Susini] stood still, peering into the dusk where he sat. Then he read a poem called "Verfall," the first poem in Georg Trakl's *Die Dichtungen*. It was as though the sea had entered the class at the last moment. For this poem was not like any poem I had ever recognized: the poet, at a sign from the evening bells, followed the wings of birds that became a train of pious pilgrims who were continually vanishing into the clear autumn of distances; beyond the distances there were black horses leaping in red maple trees, in a world where seeing and hearing are not two actions, but one. I returned to that darkening room every afternoon for months, through autumn and winter, while Professor Susini summoned every poem out of Trakl's three volumes.[84]

Wright's discovery of Trakl in 1952 corresponded with Bly's discovery of the same poet in Oslo in 1956[85] and the German poet

---

84. James Wright, "A Note on Trakl," in *Twenty Poems of Georg Trakl*, trans. James Wright and Robert Bly (Madison, Minn.: Sixties Press, 1961), 8.
85. Otto and Lofsness, "An Interview with Robert Bly," 30.

introduced an early and powerful impression on both of them independently. Bly's admiration of Trakl is founded on his use of images as well as on a sense of silence in his work, a trait often associated with Bly's own poetry: "The German language has a word for deliberately keeping silence, which English does not have. Trakl uses this word 'schweigen' often. When he says 'the flowers Bend without words over the blue pond', we realise that the flowers have a voice, and that Trakl hears it. They keep their silence in the poem."[86]

Trakl's "De Profundis" is one of the five translations appearing in Wright's *Collected Poems*. It is a surrealist narrative recounting the death of an orphan-bride who works in the fields while awaiting her marriage. An unspecified tragedy interrupts her eager longing:

> On the way home
> The shepherd found the sweet body
> Decayed in a bush of thorns.

The speaker of the poem, weighted with grief, then joins the bride by sharing her fate through images:

> At night, I found myself in a pasture,
> Covered with rubbish and the dust of stars.
> In a hazel thicket
> Angels of crystal rang out once more.

One of Wright's own poems, "American Wedding," portrays the same essential narrative outline through similar imagistic apparel. A bride's preparation for marriage is cruelly cut short:

> She dreamed long of waters.
> Inland today, she wakens
> On scraped knees, lost
> Among locust thorns.

---

86. Robert Bly, "The Silence of Georg Trakl," in *Twenty Poems of Georg Trakl*, trans. Wright and Bly, 5.

The bride does not die, as she does in Trakl's poem; rather, she is consigned to a kind of living death, not unlike that which the speaker undergoes in "De Profundis."

James Wright's interest in Theodor Storm has extended to his prose as well as his verse. *Rider on the White Horse,* a selection from Storm's novels translated by him, was published in 1964. His poetry, too, has intrigued Wright, in much the same way as that of Trakl, for its placement of images which serve as psychic equivalents at the human level. Storm's "Woman Ritornelle," for example, juxtaposes three images, a "Blossoming myrtle tree," the "shrivelling winds," and a "nutmeg herb," in succeeding stanzas. Each image is associated with a private memory from the poet's past; each is found to be now irrecoverable. The reason for the elusive quality of the imaged memories is justified by the inclusion of another image in the poem's final tercet:

> Dark cypresses—
> The world is too interested in gaiety;
> It will all be forgotten.

The final stanza serves as the epigraph for one of Wright's own poems, "Goodbye to the Poetry of Calcium," from *The Branch Will Not Break.* The epigraph is modified in the second line, however, to read "The world is uneasily happy" (*Die welt ist gar zu lustig*). Wright's poem, which seems almost a companion poem in sequence to Storm's, is conspicuous in his canon because, as the title implies, it seems to point to a new and uncalcined poetry. The poem is an apostrophe to the "Mother of roots," who seems to be partially the "Dark Cypresses" of Storm's poem, the muse, and some animistic force sweeping through the universe. She remains, however, beyond the poet's power to call her name:

> If I knew the name,
> Your name, all trellises of vineyards and old fire
> Would quicken to shake terribly my
> Earth, mother of spiralling searches, terrible
> Fable of calcium, girl.

The new poetry, one of "tall ashes of loneliness" rather than calcium, remains incomplete; but, like Storm, Wright has suggested its outlines: it will be profoundly human in such a way as to include the lonely, the blind, the ineffectual. It will also reveal itself through the images of the earth: "all trellises of vineyard and old fire / Would quicken to shake terribly my / Earth."

Bly has characterized Gottfried Benn as one "considered the greatest poet in Germany on his death in 1956."[87] His rendering in English of the title poem of one of Benn's volumes, "Poems That Stand Still," exemplified what Bly most approves of in the German's work: "The images of this new poem are not a series of arguments following each other, but groups of images which come to the poem like birds to a tree, or which arrange themselves about a hidden core."[88] This poem pits the "Wise Man" against the man of "Busyness" to the detriment of the latter. In so doing, it deplores a world which finds no occasion for solitude and silence:

> To represent some party,
> Busyness,
> Travelling to, and from,
> is the distinguishing stamp of a world
> which does not see well.

Bly's personal leaning toward the landscape of introspection and solitude, the same qualities he admires in the work of many of these poets, informs almost every poem in *Silence in the Snowy Fields,* just as the scorning of "Busyness" in his second volume makes up the subject of a poem, "The Busy Man Speaks," which is more ironic than Benn's.

The workings of the European and Latin American poets, like those of the Anglo-American tradition, are not, in most cases,

---

87. "Gottfried Benn," *Fifties,* II (1959), 53.
88. *Ibid.*

consciously or deliberately absorbed. The non–Anglo-American poets, for example, seem to have had little if any direct influence on the work of William Stafford. [89] Stafford admits an interest in Spanish poetry, but denies that Bly's translations have had a significant bearing on his work: "Bly sort of confirmed an impression and gave it an emphatic backing. But the doctrines and the poems have had no effect I can feel on my own writing, unless I can reach all the way back to such poems as those in an early Mark Van Doren anthology of World Poetry, in which I always responded to certain Spanish ballads and such—old poems. Bly's campaigns I have viewed with interest and benevolence, but from the sidelines, and without any feeling of effect on my writing." [90]

It is axiomatic, however, that without the environment of this poetry, both foreign and domestic, almost all of it written in the twentieth century, the major work of the poets of the Emotive Imagination could not have been recorded. In the discussion of the origins of their contribution to American poetry, one other source remains to be considered, and it is one that has already figured prominently: the critical postulates of Robert Bly. From this background it will be possible to go on to a comprehensive investigation of the specific achievements of his own poetry, as well as that of Wright, Simpson, and Stafford.

In their preoccupation with a kind of poetry different from that being written by their contemporaries, the poets of the Emotive Imagination have also been concerned with the need for a different criticism, one which will provide a vocabulary and set of premises by which their own work can be justly evaluated. "New kinds of criticism will have to be developed in the coming years," [91]

---

89. Stafford has collaborated with Aijaz Ahmad in some translations of the nineteenth-century Indian poet Ghalib. See *Poems by Ghalib* (New York: A Hudson Review Publication, 1969). There is no evidence that Ghalib has had any influence on Stafford's own work.

90. Stafford to George Lensing, July 15, 1972.

91. Simpson, "Dead Horses and Live Issues," 521.

Simpson explicitly asserts. It is Bly, however, who has been chiefly concerned with this need: "We have had historical criticism, which was interested in Byron's club-foot. We have had New Criticism, which pores over the intellectual background of the poem. Now a third step is needed. We need a criticism which begins all over again—a criticism which attempts to distinguish what is poetry from what is not."[92]

The founding of *Fifties* by Bly and Duffy in 1958 was intended to provide the vehicle for these new critical formulations,[93] and it continues to print in every issue critical essays, most of them by Bly, frequently under the pseudonym of the omnipresent Crunk. It remains a curiously eccentric magazine: irregular in its appearance (almost four years between numbers ten and eleven), constantly aggressive in its opinion, consistently asserting not just the taste but the temperament and pertinacity of Bly himself. Though its interest and standards, some might argue, are restrictive, it is hardly insular. Translations of hundreds of poems from all over the world have appeared in its pages. Its opinions are put forth with a certain stamping of feet, but the magazine is not without humor. "Madame Tussaud's Wax Museum," a regular feature of the magazine, enshrines bathetically the wrongheaded (Robert Lowell, William Meredith, John Ciardi, John Hollander, etc.), while "The Order of the Blue Toad" is reserved for the untouchables (Robert Penn Warren and Cleanth Brooks for their *Understanding Poetry,* for example). Parodies of poems and poets are frequent, and Bly has even published an uproarious parody of his own verse by Henry Taylor. The magazine, he informs his readers, will not continue indefinitely: "We expect the magazine to fall over the finish line of #20, and promptly expire, like a three hundred year old tortoise."[94] In 1973 Bly became a colum-

92. Robert Bly, "Prose vs. Poetry," *Choice,* II (1962), 79.
93. "I imagined the magazine to be, not for the readers, but for the poets; I put it out for poets basically and therefore we didn't care about the circulation and we published as high quality criticism as we could get." Otto and Lofsness, "An Interview with Robert Bly," 31.
94. "In Future Issues," *Sixties,* X (Summer, 1968), back page.

nist for *American Poetry Review,* even as his interest in continuing the publication of *Seventies* appeared to be flagging.

Bly's critical opinions are never ambiguous and are openly biased. His pronouncements are occasionally given to extremities and oversimplifications. The reader happens upon such comments as: "The effect of English poetry of the last hundred years on American poetry has been disastrous,"[95] or "The greatest disaster that ever happened to European literature and particularly English literature was Shakespeare: he stopped it cold."[96] Notoriety and overt attack are integrally a part of Bly's method, tactics not without calculation on his part. But his penchant for the tossed-off remark leads him, at times, into contradiction. In one review of American poetry of the 1930s, for example, he dismisses Theodore Roethke for remaining obstinately in the "old lyric tradition."[97] Elsewhere, he praises Roethke highly for his resistance to that tradition.[98] The point is that Bly's is a manifesto-criticism. As a critic, he is an apologist, one who sees his role as a vindicator for the kind of poetry he prefers.

"A poem is something that penetrates for an instant into the unconscious,"[99] declares Robert Bly in a stipulative definition. The remark summarizes three principal phenomena at work in the nature of poetry as he would have it. First, it is a poetry which "penetrates" beneath the ordinary levels of rational discourse. In his more recent comments, Bly has begun to investigate certain physiological elements involved in this movement within the brain itself.[100] Because it is a poetry that is introspective, tran-

95. Robert Bly, "On English and American Poetry," *Fifties,* II (1959), 46.

96. Kingston *et al.,* "A Conversation with Robert Bly," 5.

97. Robert Bly, "Five Decades of Modern American Poetry," *Fifties,* I (1958), 38.

98. Kingston *et al.,* "A Conversation with Robert Bly," 6 and 8.

99. Bly, "A Wrong Turning in American Poetry," 47.

100. Borrowing from Arthur Koestler, Paul MacLean, Charles Fair, and others, he differentiates among three brains in the functioning of human thought: the "reptile brain," located near the base of the skull, which emits the signals of human behavior necessary for survival at the most instinctive level. This brain is enfolded by another, the "mammal brain," out of which results basic human emotions such as love or anger. Finally, the third and most recent brain in the evolutionary process is what Bly designates

quil, and profoundly personal, it is one that does not look to others in its quest for knowledge. Too often, insists Crunk, Americans have produced a "poetry of things," rather than of the self—thus accounting for the bankruptcy of the Imagist tradition, for example. In another place Bly speaks of American poets as having pursued the expansionist policies of the national identity, rather than the inwardness out of which authentic poetic sentiment is generated. One of the "great traditions" of poetry, reiterates Crunk, is precisely the "going deeply into oneself, and returning like an explorer, perhaps saddened forever, but with strange kinds of knowledge—the tradition, for instance, of Rilke and Trakl." [101] For this reason, the best school for an aspiring poet is not a workshop in creative writing, but solitude. "My advice to anyone if he wants to write is to go and live by himself for two years and not talk to anyone." [102]

The poem, according to Bly's definition quoted above, penetrates "for an instant" the unconscious. This second element, the fact that the poem is temporary and instantaneous in its touch with the unconscious, invites a certain brevity in the length of the poem. Though Bly claims that in the work of some of the foreign poets the effect is sustained "for 20 and 50 and 80 lines long," [103] the fact remains that for the poets of the Emotive Imagination the poem's length is relatively short. The means by which the unconscious is "for an instant" awakened is that of the image, or rather, the leaps from one image to the next. Bly's notion of the images was discussed earlier in his responses to Ezra Pound and Imagism. There, as was pointed out, he insists that the image is not

---

the "new brain." It "feeds itself on . . . spiritual ideas" (Roger Kingston *et al.*, "A Conversation with Robert Bly," 7) and depends inherently upon meditation and solitude (Robert Bly, "The Three Brains," *Seventies,* I (Spring, 1972), 67). The poem as Bly conceives it is addressed to the new brain, but not without competition from the other two brains which tend, he explains, to usurp the powerful and relatively untapped energy of the third brain.

101. Bly, "The Work of Robert Creeley," 14.
102. Otto and Lofsness, "An Interview with Robert Bly," 33.
103. *Ibid.*, 30.

an external picture but the key to the unconscious, the third element in Bly's definition of the poem.

To some degree all poetry addresses the unconscious by its very appeal to emotional responses which, before the reading of the poem, lay dormant. It is, however, the manner by which the unconscious is poetically addressed that distinguishes this kind of poem from others, claims Bly. The unconscious is tapped through an emotive response not distinct from an act of recognition that occurs when the unconscious is rendered startlingly conscious through the subjective linking of images. In this sense one can speak of the poetry as mythic. Bly has apologized for the imprecision of the word *unconscious* in this context: "It seems to me that the basic thing in poetry is to try to establish some kind of a channel between your conscious mind and your unconscious. The unconscious is a very bad word for it. What we are talking of is the 'unknown part of the mind.' " [104] Part of Bly's dissatisfaction with the word *unconscious* is accounted for by the fact that he is really speaking of one aspect of it. As Jung has pointed out, "We have to distinguish between a personal unconscious and an impersonal or transpersonal unconscious." It is the latter form of the unconscious, the "collective unconscious," to which Bly seems to refer. Here one finds the gathering of "primordial images," which, says Jung, "are the most ancient and the most universal 'thought-forms' of humanity. They are as much feelings as thoughts." [105]

Bly's conception of the nature of the poem is unabashedly romantic. The fecundity of the subjective life reveals itself through the poem; a pursuit that is rational or objective only leads astray. One's response to the flow between images may be couched in rational terms, but the response itself remains emotive. Bly admits that the influence of Freud and Jung has made

104. Kingston *et al.*, "A Conversation with Robert Bly," 5.
105. C. G. Jung, "On the Psychology of the Unconscious," in *Two Essays on Analytical Psychology* (New York: Meridian Books, 1953), 76.

"the new imagination" possible because "some profundity of association has entered the mind since then."[106]

In these remarks Bly begins to outline a vocabulary for speaking about the poetry of the Emotive Imagination. The widely accepted language and method of the New Criticism is singularly inappropriate to this end, he insists, because critics like Ransom and Tate regard a poem as an object, "a clock which one sets going."[107] A major corollary follows from Bly's berating the New Criticism. When a poet describes himself in a poem, he is not to be taken as a persona or dramatic hero, but, indeed, as a singular human being unafraid to speak of himself frankly and directly. This reorientation of the voice of a poem back to the poet himself focuses anew upon the personality of that voice. It is only carrying the argument one step farther to correlate the moral quality of the poet with the aesthetic quality of the poem. Bly intimates strongly that this is the case. In the essay "The Work of Donald Hall," Crunk speaks at length on the role of the poet in a middle-class society and concludes that "poetry and the middle class are incompatible."[108] It is necessary to renounce the middle class, he continues somewhat evangelically, precisely because of the transparent relation between poet and poem: "But the poet is one who devotes his whole life to poetry; it is not merely to bring poetry into one's life, but to change the whole thing into poetry, and it is possible that to do that one must leave the middle class entirely, and all its ideas and securities."[109]

The most controversial debate rising from the pages of *Fifties, Sixties, Seventies* has been the feud between Robert Bly and James Dickey. The controversy is a practical illustration of Bly's insistence upon the moral requisite of the poet himself. The original estimation of Dickey, while never without reservations, was favorable. *The Suspect in Poetry,* Dickey's first collection of criti-

106. Bly, "Five Decades of Modern American Poetry," 37.
107. Bly, "A Wrong Turning in American Poetry," 37.
108. Crunk, "The Work of Donald Hall," *Fifties,* III (1959), 44–45.
109. *Ibid.,* 45.

cism, was published by the Sixties Press in 1964. With the publication of Dickey's *Buckdancer's Choice* in 1965, however, final disenchantment set in. Bly deplored the overtones of racism in a poem like "Slave Quarters" and the inadequate remorse on the part of the speaker of "Firebombing," a poem describing bombing missions in World War II. Dickey's personal reluctance to speak out vehemently against the Vietnam War was symptomatic of his failure as a poet: "When Mr. Dickey visits college campuses for readings, he makes clear his wholehearted support of the Vietnam war. This is his business, but we must note again the unity of the man and his work."[110]

Implicit in his debate with Dickey is another premise about the nature of poetry—one which has played a major role in Bly's own verse. It is the relation between poetry and politics. It would seem that a poetry that endorses solitude and introspection, both in the preparation for the writing of poetry and the actual content thereof, would eschew involvement in the public order. Indeed, is there not even a contradiction between the call for turning inward to the solitary self through poetry and, at the same time, turning outward to the body politic? This is a charge that has been laid against Bly—especially after the 1967 appearance of *The Light Around the Body,* the poems of which are almost all topical and political. A good part of Bly's criticism is given over to the reconciliation of these apparent discordances.

In fairness to Bly, it should be noted that his commitment as a poet to the political order was not born with the Vietnam War. In the first issue of *Fifties* in 1958 he made it clear that the imagination of his favor would never exclude the world of politics: "There is an imagination which assembles the three kingdoms within one poem: the dark figures of politics, the world of streetcars, and the ocean world."[111]

The political poem which is propagandistic does indeed con-

110. Robert Bly, "Buckdancer's Choice," *Sixties,* IX (Spring, 1967), 78.
111. Bly, "Five Decades of Modern American Poetry," 39.

tradict the poem of the inner life; the poem which is didactic in
that its first purpose is to elicit anger, horror or repulsion against
an act of the state is not a poem but a manifesto. In his essay "On
Political Poetry," written in 1967 when protests against the
Vietnam War were at their peak, Bly warns against just such a
poetry: "A true political poem is a quarrel with ourselves, as a
personal poem is, and rhetoric is as pointless in that sort of poem
as in the personal one. The true political poem does not order us
either to take any specific act; like the personal poem, it moves to
deepen awareness." [112] What Bly seems to suggest is that, while a
political poem does not aspire to move its reader to action, it does
enlarge his sensitivity and understanding of the issue. In direct-
ing the reader inward to himself, the poem does not remove him
from the great social unit of which he is a part; rather, "the good
political poem entangles in a similar way some of the psychic life
of the nation." [113]

Bly's admiration of Pablo Neruda is founded partially on the
Chilean poet's capacity to embark with the reader on a journey
into the self, leading him to the discovery that the nation's
psychic life is a part of his own. The counterpoint between the
inner and outer worlds preserves Neruda from the unrooted,
directionless world of the surrealists. [114] Any poem, as Bly would
have it, is always at odds with the complacent and commonplace.
Just as its images awaken rather than soothe, so too must its
content: "The poem devoid of any revolutionary feeling, in politics or language, has no choice but to become descriptive prose,
sociological prose—or worse, light verse." [115]

If poetry can make men meditative, introspective, and aware,
then it can make them alert to the mendacious. It is in this sense
that a "poem can be a political act." [116] The probings of the inner

---

112. Robert Bly, "On Political Poetry," *Nation*, CCIV (April 24, 1967), 523.
113. *Ibid.*, 522.
114. Bly, "The Surprise of Neruda," 19.
115. Bly, "A Wrong Turning in American Poetry," 44.
116. Robert Bly, "Leaping Up Into Political Poetry," in Bly (ed.), *Forty Poems Touching on Recent American History* (Boston: Beacon Press, 1970), 9.

world must maintain their liaison with the outer. The channel between the two worlds then protects the individual from immunity to the larger abuses of society. The individual psyche and the national psyche cannot be impervious to each other: "The poet's main job is to penetrate that husk around the American psyche, and since that psyche is inside *him* too, the writing of political poetry is like the writing of personal poetry, a sudden drive by the poet inward."[117] When Bly was awarded the National Book Award for *The Light Around the Body* in 1968, he turned over the thousand-dollar award to the draft resistance movement. The public statement wherein he announced that decision pointed to his recognition of a chasm between the inner resources of the poet and the actions of the society in which he lives—a chasm which for poetry is fatal: "These concerns are not unconnected to such a ceremony as this. For if the country is dishonored, where will it draw its honor from to give to its writers?"[118]

Two conclusions can be drawn from Bly's defense of the political poem. The first is that in the actual writing of a poem, about, say, the secretary of state in Lyndon Johnson's cabinet, it is exceedingly difficult to direct the reader inward into his own psyche and toward "awareness" rather than outward toward ridicule or scorn at the political official. Few poets have been markedly successful in writing a body of political poems. The second conclusion is another modification of the New Critical attitude toward the poem. Just as Bly insists that the poet as a man is never detached from his poem, so too is the content of the poem never removed from the affairs of the larger world. In this sense, the political poem is not a self-contained artistic entity, but it directs the reader inward to himself wherein the "deeper awareness" propels him abruptly outward to the world beyond. Far from being an independent object, the poem turns out to be a collection of images which float the reader inward to himself and outward to the society of which he is a part. The boundaries between the poem and poet, or, at the other end, the poem and the world, are never impenetrable. The poem is not an object but a process.

Bly's critical pronouncements are varied, but always lively. They inevitably direct the reader toward his own verse (indirectly) or the verse toward which he is partial (directly). As an editor, however, he has been more than a critical spokesman. Beginning with the first issue of *Fifties* in 1958, Bly has offered pages for the publication, not only of his own criticism and translations, but also for poetry. He has consistently sought out the work of younger and lesser-known poets whose work has earned his commendation, as well as better-known poets like Wright and Simpson. In 1972, Bly was instrumental in setting up the Minnesota Writers Publishing House for the publication of Minnesota poets whose work was largely unknown. With the publications financed, printed, and distributed by the poets themselves, Bly acknowledged in 1974 that he was "guiding the first ten books through the press"[119] and then planned to surrender the operation to the contributing poets.

The origins of the Emotive Imagination are complex and diverse. The use, for example, of images and personifications is traceable to the indefinite past. Obviously, the Imagist movement in the early part of the century has been central. The poetic tradition of Pound and Eliot, while in many ways distinct from the contemporary poets, has offered valuable methods and motifs. Freudian and Jungian psychologies have been powerful forces. It remains, however, impossible to speak of the emergence of the Emotive Imagination in America during the 1950s and 1960s without reference to Robert Bly. His influence has been irrepressible. As a translator of poets otherwise relatively unknown to

119. Robert Bly, "Starting a Cooperative House," *The American Poetry Review* (March/April, 1974), 13.

Americans, he has inserted other traditions of poetry into the mainstream. As an editor he has been indefatigable in broadcasting his poetics. His poetry, honored with national acclaim, is the subject of examination in the succeeding pages. Taken altogether, Robert Bly is the single individual who has been essential to the evolvement of the Emotive Imagination.

Part II Poetry of the Emotive Imagination

1 Robert Bly

THE STIMULUS injected by Robert Bly into the poets of the Emotive Imagination has not been solely as translator, editor, and theoretician. *Silence in the Snowy Fields,* a 1962 collection of poems which had appeared earlier over a period of almost ten years in the magazines, was the first volume demonstrating extensively the realized potentialities of the Emotive Imagination. Bly's second volume, *The Light Around the Body,* demonstrated his expanding interest in political poetry. The 1973 volumes *Jumping Out of Bed* and *Sleepers Joining Hands* disclose his enduring predilection for the Emotive Imagination, even as the political poems have diminished as a result of America's disengagement in Vietnam.

Bly's success as a poet depends of course on the quality of the individual poems, but, as demonstrated in Part I, his own work has been indisputably shaped by his long interest in and translation of poets like Neruda and Trakl. Moreover, his poetry also inevitably becomes a kind of illustration of his own poetics, outlined, as we have also seen, in scores of essays and reviews. When Bly says, for example, that a poem is "something that penetrates for an instant into the unconscious," one expects his own verse to show how that is so.

Unlike Wright, Simpson, and Stafford, Bly seems to have

discarded the use of rhyme and regular meters very early in his career. His poetic interest in issues of social and political import is also apparent from his earlier poems. "Choral Stanza," appearing in a 1953 issue of the *Paris Review* ("I've seen the bodies broken in the Asian streets"), holds no specific government accountable, but is indeed prophetic in its anticipation of the "turbulence of death" in Asia.

Coincidentally, the Spring, 1958, issue of the *Paris Review* contains poems by Bly, Wright, Simpson, and Stafford. The poems are noteworthy because they appear at a time when experimentation on the part of all four with the new kind of verse was still inchoate and tentative. As might be expected, Bly's poem is the only one written with no fixed metrical pattern. Only Stafford's "Requiem" is, like Bly's poem, without rhyme; Simpson's "Old Soldier" follows a regular *a b a b* rhyme scheme, while Wright's "To L., Asleep" combines both full and half rhymes. Of the four, Stafford's "Requiem" is closest to his mature style as a poet; it was included four years later in *Traveling through the Dark*. However, "The Fire of Despair Has Been Our Saviour," extensively revised in *The Light Around the Body,* is closest to the presentation of the Emotive Imagination. The earlier version seeks to disclose the sense of despair through a series of autumnal images—most of which are fairly conventional, a few cliché-ridden ("like a ship sinking"). Some are more successful:

> This autumn, instants
> Of despair are deep
> And hard to find for us, for in the woods at the end
> Of roads is despair, yet the things that we must grasp,
> The signs of the road are gone, hidden by spring and fall, leaving
> A still sky here, a dusk there,
> A dry cornleaf in the field.

One of the earliest poems selected by Bly to appear in *Silence in the Snowy Fields* is "Where We Must Look for Help." It had appeared some nine years earlier, again in the *Paris Review*. With its reappearance in the volume, the poem is found intact with only minor punctuational alterations, though the title is changed and a second stanza deleted entirely. The poem is somewhat atypical in its use of allusion—the Genesis story of the flood and Noah's sending forth doves and a raven. Nonetheless, the allusion remains in the background as Bly's poem juxtaposes the flight of three birds from the "ark eaves." The first, the dove, returns having "found no resting place." The split-tail swallows are then dispatched; they shall return, the poem indicates, but transformed as "blue swallows." Finally, the crow itself will be sent: "The crow, the crow, the spider-colored crow, / The crow shall find new mud to walk upon." What strikes the reader of this 1953 poem is the manner in which Bly uses the bird images. The later title gives the clue to their meaning—where we must look for help; the answer is contained only in the images. The birds suggest a reductive process in the pursuit of safety from peril: from the dove to the split-tail swallows to the spider-colored crow. Similarly, the flight of the various birds moves from "above the shaken seas" to the "new mud." The images imply a movement from the ethereal to the earthly, from the impossible to the credible—perhaps from the divine to the human. Although they are not "deep" in that they send the reader inward toward his own unconscious reserves, the images do function entirely by leaps from one to the other without the intervention of narrative explanation. To this degree, the poem denotes Bly's interest in this method almost a decade before his first volume.

Silence in the Snowy Fields appeared two years after William Stafford's 1960 volume *West of Your City,* and Stafford's collection had contained poems like "Vacation," as well as others, which demonstrated the ranges of the Emotive Imagination. *Traveling through the Dark,* Stafford's second volume, was issued in 1962, the same year as Bly's collection. Simpson's *At the End of the Open Road* and Wright's *The Branch Will Not Break* appeared the following year, 1963—both volumes disclosing a familiarity with the new kind of poetry. Like Stafford, both Wright and Simpson had indicated that they were moving in this direction in earlier work; obviously, many of the poems in the two 1963 volumes were written before the publication of Bly's collection. Bly's 1962 volume, however, appears to have been the first gathering of poems devoted exclusively to poetic experiments within the limits of the Emotive Imagination. For this reason, *Silence in the Snowy Fields* merits particular attention.

Some of the attributes of the poetry have already been touched upon. Bly's frequent outbursts of strong emotive self-expression ("I am happy in this ancient place") have been compared with similar statements by Neruda. His repetition of lines and phrases was compared with Vallejo's, just as his use of the long, conversational titles is not unlike Jiménez' phrasing of titles. Many of the poems of Gunnar Ekelöf share with those of Bly a setting of winter richly suffused with images and frequent personification of the natural scene. Many of these latter qualities are also to be found in the work of Trakl.

The poems of *Silence in the Snowy Fields* are very much of a world. They are not posited on moments of urgent circumstance, at least exteriorly. The poet often pictures himself in corn fields or farm houses; the drama of the poem, exteriorly, is nothing more than the approach of darkness or falling asleep or awaking or driving the car from city to city. The force of the poem consequently depends upon the establishment of a sense of intense subjectivity within these contexts of the commonplace. In each case the invasion of the psyche by a sudden moment of insight, almost a revelation, occurs with the poet most often in a state of solitude and in conjunction with some element of the natural world.

The poems are born of whimsy and casual encounter; they aim at definition of mood, which is of itself almost always evanescent. The language is colloquial—sometimes that of short, clipped, almost flat statements ("I am driving; it is dusk"), in other poems much looser and more lyrically effusive ("Shouts rise from the harbor of the blood, / Mist, and masts rising, the knock of wooden tackle in the sunlight"). The poems identify specific towns and states and seasons—most often northern midwestern states; almost always winter. The participial titles, frequently keys with which to unlock the associative pattern of the images, induce a sense of drifting motion, a suspension of time ("Driving to Town Late to Mail a Letter," "After Drinking All Night with a Friend, We Go Out In a Boat at Dawn to See Who Can Write the Best Poem," "Remembering In Oslo the Old Picture of the Magna Carta").

The combination of these attributes within a poem tends to release the mind from intensive concentration; the poems are open, lethargically available to the world and to the interior self. Recognizing this quality in Bly's work, William Heyen has remarked, "For years I felt that Bly's poetry pointed at a mysterious and dissatisfying nothingness that was a non-subject." [1] The state of lethargy, however, is a prelude to a sudden reversal: the images converge, in the best poems, both for the poem's speaker and for the reader in a moment of new knowledge.

Several of the poems of *Silence in the Snowy Fields* are organized, not by a chronological progression in narrative continuity, but by a retrogression through time. The human mind, responding to images and finding itself thrust inward upon itself, is also thrust into the remote past. Poems like "Return to Solitude," "Surprised by Evening," "Unrest," "Summer, 1960, Minnesota," "On the Ferry Across Chesapeake Bay," and others surrealistically depict, or at least yearn for, a return to one's ancient origins. In almost every case these poems rely heavily on sea imagery, disclosing what Anthony Piccione calls "a type of cellular memory of all existence." [2]

"Afternoon Sleep" is a representative poem from Bly's first

---

1. William Heyen, "Inward to the World, The Poetry of Robert Bly," *The Far Point,* III (Fall/Winter, 1969), 43.
2. Anthony Piccione, "Robert Bly and the Deep Image" (Ph.D. dissertation, Ohio University, 1970), 98.

volume in its use of images and the leaps among them terminating in a kind of epiphany. The sixteen-line poem is divided into three stanzas and begins, typically, with the first moments of consciousness after sleep. The speaker's dream, "my wife, / And the loneliness hiding in grass and weeds," is reimpressed upon his waking mind—"and suddenly enters." The remainder of the poem seems to have no logical connection with the first stanza. It describes in deliberately undramatic terms a ride out to the abandoned farm of a friend, Joe Sjolie, who one day abruptly disappeared. Left in the farmhouse is his "bachelor rocker." Sjolie's dog is presumably dead: "He refused to take food from strangers." The poem concludes with a deliberate flatness:

> When I climbed the porch, the door was open.
> Inside were old abandoned books,
> And instructions to Norwegian immigrants.

The poem as narrative seems to have no point at all: a nap followed by a visit to an abandoned farmhouse. The poem's meaning, however, is contained in something else. The loose arrangement of details, one discovers, is not arbitrary. The dream itself has been one of loneliness that has carried over into the world of consciousness. The poet's loneliness inevitably links up with the loneliness of the Norwegian immigrant. Sjolie's isolation emerges solely through images: the bachelor rocker, the farm "sheltered" by trees, the society-resisting dog. Even in the line "The matted grass lay around the house," the sense of boundary and division is calmly reinforced—especially in conjunction with "the loneliness hiding in grass and weeds" from the earlier dream description. These images are ignited with the last lines—particularly the "instructions to Norwegian immigrants" found inside the empty house. Sjolie's isolation becomes complete: he is a foreigner, an old man, someone who has mysteriously disappeared. At no point does the poet define his personal relationship to Sjolie, but his own dream of loneliness which induced him, upon awakening, to visit the farm implies a sense of failed responsibility on the part of the poet toward Sjolie. The poem is successful, however, because the images themselves define this human relationship; narrative exposition would be noisily redundant.

When the English poet Thom Gunn reviewed Bly's volume in the *Yale Review* in 1963, he was basically unsympathetic, though perceptive of Bly's method. He speaks of Bly's use of the image as "sole repository of the poem's meaning," but objects to the notion that "the presentation of things is sufficient meaning in itself." He also deplores "a world of total innocence, without evil, and simply for enjoyment." Gunn is not altogether just in calling Bly's world innocent, as the various psychological overtones of a poem like "Afternoon Sleep" attest. Bly's awareness of a world of evil, however, became incontrovertible with the publication of *The Light Around the Body* in 1967, the volume for which he was given the National Book Award.

The landscape of the poems of the second volume shifts from the snowy cornfields of Madison, Minnesota, to the councils of state in Washington, and the lethargic state of peaceful communion with nature is converted to a melancholy and occasionally petulant exposure of an immoral government. The temperate poem becomes baldly topical; irony issues as a more potent weapon. The specific controversy which underlies *The Light Around the Body* is America's involvement in the Vietnam War, an issue seen in conjunction with the racism and poverty throughout the society. In this context, even the volume's title assumes a certain irony. The use of personifications also changes from the first to the second volume: from "Tiny birds are singing / In the secluded prairies / And in the deep valleys of the hand" (" 'Taking the Hands' ") to "Chrysanthemums crying out on the borders of death" ("Smothered by the World").

Though Bly's interest in the political poem and his awareness of the socially disadvantaged are apparent from his earlier poems, it is clear that during the middle and late 1960s a shift in the nature of his work occurred. The moralist tended to replace the lyricist. This is not to suggest that the poems of *The Light Around the Body* are without lyricism; indeed, the value of examining this volume is precisely to show the workings of the Emotive Imagination within the context of the political poem.

Images remain central in the political poems, but the images tend to crowd the poem in a more heterogeneously surrealistic fashion. The earlier poems generally contain the outline of narrative; most of the political poems abandon narrative and are more erratically discursive. "War and Silence," for example, begins:

> The bombers spread out, temperature steady
> A Negro's ear sleeping in an automobile tire
> Pieces of timber float by saying nothing
>
> Bishops rush about crying, There is no war.

Even punctuation has been shunned in this mélange of imagery.

Animal and nature imagery makes up a part of almost every poem in the second volume, but to ends different from those of the earlier volume. If the setting of summer in Minnesota is tranquil and benign, in "Driving through Minnesota during the Hanoi Bombings" for example, that serenity is intended only as an ironic contrast to the Asian horrors. In this sense, the poem does not send the reader inward to himself, but outward to the urgency of the war. Consequently, the images of Minnesota and Asia do not coalesce but repel, and the attempt in the poem to merge the two worlds is less than convincing:

> Our own gaiety
> Will end up
> In Asia, and in your cup you will look down
> And see
> Black Starfighters.

In other poems the nature imagery is itself radically different. If in the first volume there occasionally appeared an image of the unsavory, it was magically (though sometimes crudely) transformed: "A dream of moles with golden wings / Is not so bad"

("Laziness and Silence"). With the first poem in *The Light Around the Body,* "The Executive's Death," the moles reappear, but now clearly with no movement toward metamorphosis. The morally callous commuters of the poem arrive home "like moles / Or hares flying from a fire behind them." The difference suggests that the hideous has triumphed over the comely—a premise that could only presage major change for the Emotive Imagination.

"Counting Small-Boned Bodies" is a short poem of ten lines and, as its title suggests, plays upon official body counts of dead Vietnamese soldiers. The poem's first line, "Let's count the bodies over again," is followed by three tercets, each of which begins with the same line: "If we could only make the bodies smaller." That condition granted, Bly postulates three successive images: a plain of skulls in the moonlight, the bodies "in front of us on a desk," and a body fit into a finger ring which would be, in the poem's last words, "a keepsake forever." One notes in this that Bly uses imagery not unlike that of the pre-Vietnam poems, especially in the image of the moonlit plain. In fact, that very image functions here ironically as the reader perceives that the romantic setting is occupied by the skulls. Bly's method consequently represents an important modification in the use of the Emotive Imagination. The lyricism that attends the natural world has become an ironic lyricism attending horrible reversals of the natural world. The reader, instead of drifting tranquilly inward and toward his own private world, is thrust outward upon the abuses of the public world. The poem does not end in reconciliation or a sense of moral advance; rather, it concludes upon a note of accusation and a sense of moral retrogression.

One of the connections in the use of the imagination between the first two volumes by Bly is his incorporation of American history. Bly does not use it often in either volume, but it is a subject that has long appealed to him.[3] In a poem like "Hatred of

3. See Robert Bly (ed.), *Forty Poems Touching on Recent American History* (Boston: Beacon Press, 1970).

Men with Black Hair," from *The Light Around the Body,* the first
four stanzas are only the most thinly veiled of diatribes. The last
stanza, however, sharply reverses the anger and offers perhaps
the finest lines in the second volume as it introduces the figure of
the American Indian:

> Underneath all the cement of the Pentagon
> There is a drop of Indian blood preserved in snow:
> Preserved from a trail of blood that once led away
> From the stockade, over the snow, the trail now lost.

Taken as a whole, *The Light Around the Body* appears somewhat dated today. The poems from Bly's first volume appealed to a
shared and universal consciousness between poet and reader. His
second, however, sought to shock the reader into a new consciousness, one that would lead him to political reaction. Such
ambition occasionally fosters propaganda, while the shrillness of
many of the poems is muted, if at all, by irony.

In 1970, Kayak Books published Bly's *The Morning Glory,*
which consists of twenty prose poems (the title page declares that
there are twelve), none of them ostensibly political in nature.
Three years later, Barre Publishers issued a collection of twenty
short poems by Bly, *Jumping Out of Bed.* Though these volumes
received relatively little critical attention upon publication, they
mark a reorientation in the work of Bly. Here there are no allusions to Vietnam, the Pentagon, or the guilt of being an American
citizen. In fact, the landscape and attitude of these poems return
to the more private and more innocent world of *Silence in the
Snowy Fields.*

"Like the New Moon I Will Live My Life," the third lyric in
Jumping Out of Bed, is a reaffirmation of the basic qualities of the
Emotive Imagination, most of which are present to a greater or
lesser extent in the other poems in this collection:

> When your privacy is beginning over,
> how beautiful the things are that you did not notice before!
> A few sweetclover plants

along the road to Bellingham,
culvert ends poking out of driveways,
wooden corncribs, slowly falling,
what no one loves, no one rushes toward or shouts about,
what lives like the new moon,
and the wind
blowing against the rumps of grazing cows.

Telephone wires stretched across water,
a drowning sailor standing at the foot of his mother's bed,
grandfathers and grandsons sitting together.

In the first stanza Bly aligns images of "things . . . you did not notice before." Each is taken as an illustration of "your privacy . . . beginning over." The objects are rural and unobtrusive: sweetclover plants, culvert ends, corncribs, and "the wind / blowing against the rumps of grazing cows." These images take on meaning, however, only with the three concluding lines.

At first glance, there appears to be little if any connection between these lines and the objects of stanza one. One notes, however, that the telephone wires, the drowning sailor, and the grandfathers are all engaged in acts of reaching out toward human communication. In addition, each draws subtly from a preceding image: the drowning sailor is associated with the water over which the telephone wires stretch; the mother's bed draws together the generations of grandfathers and grandsons in the poem's final line. The poem's title, "Like the New Moon I Will Live My Life," declares the moral purport toward which all the images point: renewal ("privacy is beginning over"), integration of the self with the simple and ordinary ("what no one loves, no one rushes toward or shouts about"), and finally human reconciliation in the concluding lines. The process here, while it suggests the programmatic, is not explicit except through the relationship of the images. The poet's attitude is conveyed solely through his ordering of the images and his act of faith in their ability to draw potency from the surrounding images. Meaning is cumulative and emerges through emotive inference.

Other poems of *Jumping Out of Bed* reassert Bly's earlier and cherished tenets of the Emotive Imagination: *personifications of nature:* "It may be the trees I see have consciousness / and this desire to weep comes from them" ("Some November Privacy Poems"); *human privacy:* "This water falls like a great privacy" ("Sleeping Faces"); *solitude:* "Each day I did not spend in solitude was wasted" ("After Long Busyness"); *outward passivity:* "How magnificent to be doing nothing, / moving aimlessly through a nighttime field, / and the body alive, like a plant!" ("Chrysanthemums").

A larger and more ambitious volume, *Sleepers Joining Hands,* was issued in 1973 by Harper & Row. The volume reprints one poem, "Six Winter Privacy Poems," from *Jumping Out of Bed* and the longest poem in the collection, "The Teeth Mother Naked At Last," had appeared three years earlier in the Pocket Poets series of City Lights Books. *Sleepers Joining Hands* also contains over twenty pages of prose under the title "I Came Out of the Mother Naked." The latter, a sweeping and at times fanciful essay, is a strongly Jungian account of the loss of the cultural and psychological dominance of "the Great Mother" after being overridden by the "father consciousness" about four thousand years ago. Bly perceives, however, that the shift from the feminine to the masculine domination in values now seems to be reversing itself: "The return to the Mother as a mass movement began in the late fifties." He sees the return as a mixed blessing. Instead of the humanizing qualities of feminine virtue, the influence of the Teeth Mother portends the more perilous: "But the Vietnam war has helped everyone to see how much of the Teeth Mother there is in the United States. The culture of affluence opens the psyche to the Teeth Mother and the Death Mother in ways that no one understands."

Much like Yeats's rough beast, the image of the Teeth Mother is introduced as the cataclysmic emblem of the future at the end of Bly's long poem, "The Teeth Mother Naked At Last."

Bly's composition is more topical and less mythic than "The Second Coming," however, and in many ways the poem is an anomaly in *Sleepers Joining Hands*. Besides its initial publication three years earlier (from which some minor changes were made), it was written before the end of America's participation in the Vietnamese war. It is Robert Bly's most vehement outcry against the war and American complicity in it.

The method of the poem is simple and not unlike many anti-war poems of the 1960s: the rounding-up by cynical blame-laying of all Americans into the camp of war. Sarcasm and derision propel the poem's argument. It is the hands of the government's leaders that are perhaps most bloody, but the leaders are not alone. Teachers and churchmen are implicated: "The ministers lie, the professors lie, the television lies, the priests lie." Middle-class affluence fuels the atrocities: "The Marines use cigarette lighters to light the thatched roofs of huts / because so many Americans own their own homes." Even the personae of the American past are co-conspirators: "This is Hamilton's triumph. / This is the advantage of a centralized bank. / B–52s come from Guam." In its relentless rhetoric of carping, the poem suggests more the poet's own catharsis than "a quarrel with ourselves," the condition that Bly had named in 1967 as necessary to "a true political poem."[4]

"Teeth Mother Naked At Last" is Whitmanesque in the use of sprawling and oracular lines which constitute catalogues of denunciation, such as the presidential lies in Part II. The poet himself assumes the role of the Civil War nurse of Whitman's *Drum Taps:* "the staff sergeant from North Carolina is dying— you hold his hand." Bly's poem should be read in the context of *The Light Around the Body* and his other antiwar verse; it echoes Simpson's method of shock in "The Inner Part."

With the exception of "Conditions of the Working Classes:

---

4. Bly, "On Political Poetry," 523.

1970," the other poems in *Sleepers Joining Hands* are not ostensibly political, and, like the poems of *Jumping Out of Bed,* they resituate the poet in various settings of isolation and calm. Most are fewer than twenty lines in length and all employ images phantasmagorically.

The last four poems of the volume, however, grouped under the subtitle "Sleepers Joining Hands," give evidence of poetry somewhat different from Bly's earlier work. Each of the four is longer than Bly's customary length and each is structured on a dream sequence involving a psychic journey. As in his early work, Bly uses a procession of imagery in a surreal fashion, but the poem's impact depends less on the stark juxtaposition of the images leading the reader to the sudden shock of personal recognition. The element of shock or abrupt insight, in fact, plays no role in these poems. Instead, the reader finds himself carried along in a stream of images identifying the speaker of the poem with all forms of matter: mineral, vegetable, animal, pre- and post-evolutionary. The following passage is from the fourth of the four poems, "Water Drawn Up Into the Head":

> When the waterholes go, and the fish flop about
> in the caked mud, they can moisten each other faintly.
>   That is good, but best
> is to let them lose themselves in a river.
> So rather than saying that Christ is God or he is not,
> it is better to forget all that
> and lose yourself in the curved energy.
> I entered that energy one day,
> that is why I have lived alone in old places,
> that is why I have knelt in churches, weeping,
> that is why I have become a stranger to my father.
> We have no name for you, so we say:
> he makes grass grow upon the mountains,
> and gives food to the dark cattle of the sea,
> he feeds the young ravens that call on him.

Theodore Roethke's later poetry hovers unmistakably around these poems—especially his poems of the *North American Se-*

quence. In "Meditation at Oyster River," for example, some of Roethke's lines are not far removed from Bly's expression:

> In this hour,
> In this first heaven of knowing,
> The flesh takes on the pure poise of the spirit,
> Acquires, for a time, the sandpiper's insouciance,
> The hummingbird's surety, the kingfisher's cunning—
> I shift on my rock, and I think:
> Of the first trembling of a Michigan brook in April,
> Over a lip of stone, the tiny rivulet;
> And that wrist-thick cascade tumbling from a cleft rock.

The incantatory tone of these lines and the repetition of words at the beginning of lines are also employed by Bly. Bly's losing himself in the "curved energy" of primitive life is not unlike Roethke's assumption of the "pure poise of spirit." For each, the psyche's fixity in nature is of a religious nature and both hint of union with primordial streams.

In the past quarter-century of Bly's publication of poetry, he appears to have found reinforcements of and elaborations upon a fundamental method which sprang up almost at once in his work and which was clearly worked out by the time of his first volume in 1962, *Silence in the Snowy Fields.* He has not departed radically from the use of the Emotive Imagination as we have defined it, and his work, perhaps more than the other poets treated here, represents a continuing and long-range experimentation with its resources. Most of Bly's poems are whimsical and minor; they have no pretensions of being anything else. Frequently his political verse manages to go little beyond bald propaganda. His poetry finally belongs in the same context as his translations, as well as his criticism and editing. As an indefatigable man-of-letters, in the best sense of the term, Robert Bly has been a vital phenomenon in American poetry since mid-century.

2 James Wright

BOTH James Wright and Louis Simpson markedly alter their methods of composition at the end of the 1950s and beginning of the 1960s. To understand the extent to which these changes represent new departures, it is necessary to pay attention to the earlier poems, which comprise two fine canons written almost within the conventions of rhyme, meter, and stanza divisions.

In the prefatory remarks to his first volume, *The Green Wall* (1957), a Yale Series of Younger Poets selection, James Wright comments that he wanted to emulate the manner of Edwin Arlington Robinson and Robert Frost, and further, that he "wanted to make the poems say something humanly important instead of just showing off with language." To a limited extent, these poems suggest Frost's manner of calm, direct statement; but more important, the poems in *The Green Wall* and to a greater extent those in his second volume, *Saint Judas* (1959), do indeed have sources both in subject matter and in method in the work of Robinson. Although the "showing off with language" that Wright eschews is ironically a charge leveled at *The Green Wall* in Bly's "The Work of James Wright," Ralph J. Mills, Jr., in a 1964 essay first published in the *Chicago Review,* describes the success

Wright has had in attaining the objectives he shares with Frost and Robinson:

> In that initial book, and in his second one, *Saint Judas* (1959), the poet sets himself to this task through poems that are meditations on his own experience, observations of other lives, dramatic situations; his speech is direct, his sympathy and judgment are undisguised. The world called up by his imagination in poetry is unmistakably the one we know, in which people are born, endure pain, discover love, encounter success or defeat in their efforts, and go down to death. It is not a symbolic world or a self-contained poetic cosmos, but a reality composed of men and women, of animals and birds, of stones, and trees, and is usually located in the American Midwest, in Ohio and Minnesota where Wright has spent so much time. [1]

Certainly the subject of death—except for *The Branch Will Not Break* (1963), Wright's most important volume—has been a constant one for Wright; in fact, one is correct in saying that of all American poets (Edgar Lee Masters excepted), past or present, there is no one obsessed with death to the degree evident in the poetry of Wright. Frankly, there are too many poems that in one way or another treat death to permit individual discussion. It will suffice to provide a selective listing of titles taken from *The Green Wall* alone: "On the Skeleton of a Hound," "Three Steps to the Graveyard," "Father," "Elegy in a Firelit Room," "Arrangements with Earth for Three Dead Friends," "A Poem about George Doty in the Death House," "To a Fugitive," "A Gesture by a Lady with an Assumed Name," "The Angel, " and "The Assignation."

Several of these poems merit brief attention for the death motif; others will be discussed later in different contexts. "Three Steps to the Graveyard" is about the speaker's father and is structured metaphorically, each stanza concerning different perspectives distanced by time and seasonal change. "Father" is a moving, surrealistic treatment of the relationship of a father and son.

---

1. Ralph J. Mills, Jr., *Contemporary American Poetry* (New York: Random House, 1965), 198.

The speaker, the son, is talking as if he were dead in "paradise," as he tells us in the first line of the poem. "Father" ends simply, but the emotion conveyed is genuine: "He drew me from the boat. I was asleep. / And we went home together." Both "The Angel" and "The Assignation" employ the same technique as that of "Father": the speaker is a ghost who returns to earth, in each instance to see what happened after the speaker's death. And both poems work with the subject of love and the theme of betrayal.

With *The Branch Will Not Break* and *Two Citizens* (1973) as exceptions, Wright's poetry deals extensively with characters on the fringe or outside of what most people define as "normal" society. Prostitutes, drunkards, bums, and criminals abound in his poetry, as well as what we might call ordinary human beings who are lonely and alienated in large measure from the rest of society. As Stephen Stepanchev says in *American Poetry Since 1945*: "[In *The Green Wall*] he writes about people, about simple, desperate, unhappy people like those who populate the poems of Edwin Arlington Robinson and Robert Frost."[2] And Mills notices that Wright's characters' actions "have transgressed the conventions of the community" and, as a result, they "are converted into scapegoats of society." Mills comments further: "With other modern poets as dissimilar as E. E. Cummings and Stanley Kunitz, Wright takes the side of the alienated individual, the hunted and persecuted, and opposes the impersonal majority or the monolithic state."[3]

In 1952/53, Wright had a Fulbright grant to study in Vienna. Crunk writes that during this time the poet was introduced to the poetry of Georg Trakl, an introduction that, in some measure, was instrumental in prompting Wright's later abandonment of the conventions in favor of a looser, more colloquially based style

2. Stephen Stepanchev, *American Poetry Since 1945* (New York: Harper & Row, 1965), 182.
3. Mills, *Contemporary American Poetry*, 200–201.

that relied on the efficacy of images and on the exciting use of tropes. At any rate, Crunk comments that when Wright compared the poems he had been writing to those by Trakl, "he came to the conclusion that his own work was not actually poetry; it had not helped anyone else to solitude, and had not helped him toward solitude."[4] Wright's own concern with poetry's "helping" is not unlike that expressed by Robinson in two letters dated respectively May 13, 1896, and February 3, 1897, to Harry de Forest Smith. Here are the pertinent excerpts:

If printed lines are good for anything, they are bound to be picked up some time; and then, if some poor devil of a man or woman feels any better or any stronger for anything that I have said, I shall have no fault to find with the scheme or anything in it.

I also make free to say that many of my verses [were] written with a conscious hope that they might make some despairing devil a little stronger and a little better satisfied with things—not as they are, but as they are to be.[5]

Indeed, Wright may well have been drawn to his primary character types by those Robinson chose, since his admiration for the older poet is great and his imitation of Robinson's method is apparent in certain of his poems, particularly those from *Saint Judas*.

The concluding lines to "The Fishermen," a poem in which the speaker, accompanied by a friend, is walking along a seacoast, describe effectively the physical characteristics and the psychic conditions of the old fishermen, for whom the speaker has understanding and compassion, two qualities everywhere apparent in the poetry of Robinson:

> Saurian faces still as layered lime,
> The nostrils ferned in smoke behind their pipes,

4. Crunk, "The Work of James Wright," *Sixties*, IV (Fall, 1960), 59.
5. Denham Sutcliffe (ed.), *Untriangulated Stars: Letters of Edwin Arlington Robinson to Harry de Forest Smith 1890–1905* (Cambridge, Mass: Harvard University Press, 1947), 247 and 273.

The eyes resting in whorls like shells on driftwood,
The hands relaxing, letting out the ropes;
And they, whispering together,
The beaten age, the dead, the blood gone dumb.

Although the fishermen are not excluded, as such, from conventional society, other characters in *The Green Wall* for whom Wright expresses unabashed sympathy are clearly beyond the definitive boundaries: George Doty, the rapist and murderer, in "A Poem about George Doty in the Death House"; the protagonist identified as Maguire in "To a Fugitive"; the lesbian who had an affair with a married woman and who was scorned by her neighbors in "Sappho"; and the prostitutes in "A Gesture by a Lady with an Assumed Name" and in "Morning Hymn to a Dark Girl."

The last two poems belong in a loosely defined sequence of love poems; both will be discussed later in this chapter: "Morning Hymn to a Dark Girl," an excellent poem, as illustrative of Wright's use of the richly rhetorical; and "Sappho" as a pre–Emotive Imagination poem. The other poems in the love sequence—"Eleutheria," "Autumnal," "The Shadow and the Real," "Witches Waken the Natural World in Spring," and "The Quail"—are descriptive lyrics in which the women are treated in images of the natural world. One senses that the women in these poems are "inserted" in order to permit the poet to write descriptively about nature. These women are only vaguely realized; the dramatic action seems to reside in the descriptive element. The closing stanza of "Witches Waken the Natural World in Spring" documents this vagueness and the image-creating nature of the poem:

> Except that spring was coming on
> Or might have come already while
> We lay beside a smooth-veined stone;
> Except an owl sang half a mile
> Away; except a starling's feather

> Softened my face beside a root:
> But how should I remember whether
> She was the one who spoke, or not?

"The Quail," another in which the woman does not possess a distinct character but rather is blended into the natural setting, does not do much more than celebrate one aspect of a relationship in a rather superficial manner, though the poem is technically impressive.

Indeed, the poems in *The Green Wall* represent high technical achievement, and Wright demonstrates more than competence in a variety of meters, in complex rhyme and near-rhyme patterns, and in stanzas in which he deftly manipulates both length and sense. Most of the poems in the volume do adhere rather strictly to the technical conventions, though Wright is not bound to them so strictly that he compromises the integrity of the poem as poem. "The Seasonless," the second poem in the book, is typical of an early Wright lyric, consisting of four stanzas of ten iambic tetrameter lines rhymed somewhat irregularly but essentially following an *a b a b c d e e c d* pattern. Concerned with the correspondence of winter to the sense of emptiness a man experiences, "The Seasonless" is rhythmically insistent, as are a number of Wright's early lyrics. He achieves this insistence through a fine command of metrics and an equally fine use of parallel structure, the latter evident in the following excerpts taken from the first and second stanzas:

> The blistered trellis seems to move
> The memory toward root and rose,
> The empty fountain fills the air
> With spray that spangled women's hair.
> . . . .
> How painlessly a man recalls
> The stain of green on crooked walls,
> The summer never known before,
> The garden heaped to bloom and fade.

Insistent rhythms gained through parallel structure in the opening lines of "A Girl in a Window"—a poem about the pleasure her
outlined figure at twilight provides for men walking by—establish
the sensuous force the poem intends:

> Now she will lean away to fold
> The window blind and curtain back,
> The yellow arms, the hips of gold,
> The supple outline fading black,
> Bosom availing nothing now,
> And rounded shadow of long thighs.

Crunk objects to Wright's "elaborate syntax" and to what he
labels Wright's "mushiness," the product of his commitments to
the conventions of syntax, in *The Green Wall* and to a lesser
extent in *Saint Judas*. These impede, according to Crunk, the "two
energies [that] have been trying to get free in James Wright's
work: the first is natural American speech, the second images."
He continues: "What prevented the natural speech [of Wright in
The Green Wall] from coming free was a nest of syntax in which
the speech became hopelessly entangled." Wright, he concludes,
"has had a heavy struggle with syntax."[6] Certainly there are
poems in *The Green Wall* in which Wright is enamored of the
lushly rhetorical, but this alone is not what Crunk finds objec-
tionable: "Despite all the voices to the contrary, the iambic meter
is not suited to the English language. The language may fall
naturally into tum de tum, as conservatives repeat at every
beaufest, but in order to maintain iambic meter, an elaborate
syntax is necessary. It is the elaborate syntax which is unnatural
in English."[7]

   "Morning Hymn to a Dark Girl" contains as many instances of
"elaborate syntax" and "mushiness" as any other poem in *The*

---

6. Crunk, "The Work of James Wright," 70–72.
7. *Ibid.*, 72.

Green Wall; yet in part because of its very lushness, which is perfectly appropriate to the subject, this lyric to a black prostitute named Betty is a remarkably successful poem. In iambic pentameter and structured by a series of contrasts, the poem begins by the speaker's negative observations of the setting in which he finds himself:

> Summoned to desolation by the dawn,
> I climb the bridge over the water, see
> The Negro mount the driver's cabin and wave
> Goodbye to the glum cop across the canal,
> Goodbye to the flat face and empty eyes
> Made human one more time. That uniform
> Shivers and dulls against the pier, is stone.

At dawn the city is a dull, aseptic sight, with buses drifting over the bridge, which is ironically called the "upper world" in contrast later to the lower, archetypal world symbolized in the dream world of Africa. "Over the lake," the speaker continues, "The windows of the rich waken and yawn"; this is a particularly apt personification.

After the speaker concludes his descriptive treatment of the pale town and its morning inhabitants, he turns his attention to Betty, whom he celebrates beginning in the seventeenth line of this forty-four-line poem:

> I celebrate you, Betty, flank and breast
> Rich to the yellow silk of bed and floors;
> Now half awake, your body blossoming trees;
> One arm beneath your neck, your legs uprisen,
> You blow dark thighs back, back into the dark.

The "dark" to which the speaker alludes is Betty's dream world, which is replete with images of her ancestry in the jungles of Africa, the dark continent that in her mind she has never left and that in her dream takes on the proportions of a mythic paradise. The pale, lifeless world of day in the American city is thus contrasted unfavorably with the lush land of her background, which in a dream allows her to escape from the "snickers" in the whorehouse where she works.

The language employed in describing Betty's dream world is rightly lush and elaborate, sensuously recreating the rich primitive life inherent in Betty, who must necessarily sleep during the daytime. The images, rhythms, and tone of these lines help to establish the clear superiority of Betty's imagined life over the real lives most of us lead. Though the following quotation is lengthy, it illustrates the exceptional quality of Wright's "elaborate syntax" properly used:

> Your shivering ankles skate the scented air;
> Betty, burgeoning your golden skin, you poise
> Tracing gazelles and tigers on your breasts,
> Deep in the jungle of your bed you drowse;
> Fine muscles of the rippling panthers move
> And snuggle at your calves; under your arms
> Mangoes and melons yearn; and glittering slowly,
> Quick parakeets trill in your heavy trees,
> O everywhere, Betty, between your boughs.
>
> Pity the rising dead who fear the dark.
> Soft Betty, locked from snickers in a dark
> Brothel, dream on; scatter the yellow corn
> Into the wilderness, and sleep all day.
> For the leopards leap into the open grass,
> Bananas, lemons fling air, fling odor, fall.
> And, gracing darkly the dark light, you flow
> Out of the grove to laugh at dreamy boys,
> You greet the river with a song so low
> No lover on a boat can hear, you slide
> Silkily to the water; where you rinse
> Your fluted body, fearless; though alive
> Orangutans sway from the leaves and gaze,
> Crocodiles doze along the oozy shore.

"Morning Hymn to a Dark Girl" proceeds by tropes, one of which is personification. In fact, Wright's use of personification has never been notably absent from his work, though its frequency increases dramatically in his poems of the Emotive Imagination in *The Branch Will Not Break*. Since Bly, Wright, Stafford, and to a lesser degree Simpson work regularly with personification, it is not surprising that the poems of the Emotive Imagination are highly metaphorical, because personifications are tropes and thus metaphoric in nature. Several examples from "Eleutheria" suffice to demonstrate Wright's use of the personification method early in his career:

> The pale cloud walking home to winter. . . .
>
> The stripping twilight plundered trees of boughs. . . .
>
> The dark began to climb the empty hill. . . .
>
> She glides lightly; the pale year follows her. . . .
>
> The moments ride away. . . .

Of the poems included in *The Green Wall,* "Sappho" is the closest in technique to the later Wright poems in the manner of the Emotive Imagination. Despite the rhythmic insistence in certain passages, the language is more colloquial than other poems in the collection, the line lengths are irregular at times, and, most important, the poem relies on metaphor more than others in *The Green Wall.* For example, the woman with whom the lesbian-speaker is having an affair is referred to as both a "blue blossom" and an apple; and the speaker at one point states directly, "Love is a cliff." Toward the end of "Sappho," the speaker discusses her situation of martyrdom and exclusion from society through the metaphoric use of fire imagery:

> I am given to burn on the dark fire they make
> With their sly voices.
>
> But I have burned already down to bone.
> There is a fire that burns beyond the names
> Of sludge and filth of which this world is made.
> Agony sears the dark flesh of the body,

> And lifts me higher than the smoke, to rise
> Above the earth, above the sacrifice;
> Until my soul flares outward like a blue
> Blossom of gas fire dancing in mid-air:
> Free of the body's work of twisted iron.

There are some, but not many, indications in the poems of *Saint Judas,* published two years after *The Green Wall,* that Wright's poetry is moving in the direction of the Emotive Imagination. Several poems—notably "All the Beautiful Are Blameless," "The Revelation," "A Prayer in My Sickness," and perhaps "At the Executed Murderer's Grave"—suggest that the poet's work is loosening up somewhat. Even though "All the Beautiful Are Blameless," in which the speaker meditates on the drowning of a woman, contains some occasional rhyming, its language is in part colloquial and conversational as these lines illustrate: "Only another drunk would say she heard / A natural voice / Luring the flesh across the water." In this poem the reader senses Wright's need for some semblance of external forms on which to fix the poem and his conflicting desire to break into a more open manner. Crunk argues that in this volume the "voices are stronger, though the syntax is often still literary," by which he means that Wright's commitment to meter impedes his natural voice from coming out freely as it does in *The Branch Will Not Break.* Crunk observes, and rightly so, that as "he writes more, Wright's poems depend less and less and less on elaborate syntax to give the illusion of form, and as the syntax retreats, hearable voices come forward."[8]

The concluding stanza of "The Revelation," an essentially iambic tetrameter, rhymed, and stanzaic poem about his father, reveals an interesting combination of formal elements and the imaginative use of metaphor:

> And weeping in the nakedness
> Of moonlight and of agony,

8. *Ibid.,* 70–71.

> His blue eyes lost their barrenness
> And bore a blossom out to me.
> And as I ran to give it back,
> The apple branches, dripping black,
> Trembled across the lunar air
> And dropped white petals on his hair.

Even more emotive is "A Prayer in My Sickness," a ten-line poem that, apart from the sameness of line length, could easily have been extracted from *The Branch Will Not Break*. Perhaps Wright felt that the speaker's delirium provided justification for the intense subjectivity of the poem. In any event, the poem is significant enough as a forerunner of the later poems to permit its reproduction here:

> You hear the long roll of the plunging ground,
> The whistle of stones, the quail's cry in the grass.
> I stammer like a bird, I rasp like stone,
> I mutter, with gray hands upon my face.
> The earth blurs, beyond me, into dark.
> Spinning in such bewildered sleep, I need
> To know you, whirring above me, when I wake.
> Come down, come down. I lie afraid.
> I have lain alien in my self so long,
> How can I understand love's angry tongue?

More so than in *The Green Wall* and therefore an indication that Wright's poetry, if not changing as such, is preparing to change, is his increased use of the personification method in *Saint Judas*. Three poems—"Sparrows in a Hillside Drift," "Dog in a Cornfield," and "The Cold Divinities"—employ at least two personifications each, and the personifications, unlike those in *The Green Wall*, are grounded firmly in the natural world, to which the following from "Dog in a Cornfield" testify: "The lazy maples wailed beyond the crust / Of earth and artificial man. / Here lay one death the autumn understands."

Yet, despite these excursions away from the manner characterizing the poems of *The Green Wall*, most of the selections in *Saint Judas* owe allegiance to prosodic conventions. "Complaint," the opening poem of the collection, is written in heroic couplets, and "Saint Judas," the closing one, is a qualified Italian sonnet. In between, Wright remains with his most comfortable thematic considerations, such as a preoccupation with death and with those alienated in contemporary society: "*Saint Judas* continues most of the interests of Wright's first book, but a more penetrating insight into the poet's own person is apparent in many of these poems. The injurious and tragic aspects of existence are examined freely, and the quality of Wright's poetic speech becomes even more direct and terse as he attempts relentlessly to locate and state the human truths that matter to him."[9] And Crunk observes that in the poems of *Saint Judas* "one can see his determination to keep the modest syntax of Robinson, at least, and still bring in the living voice."[10]

Nearly half the poems in the volume deal with the subject of death in one way or another. Perhaps the Robinson influence is in part responsible for Wright's obsessive concern with the subject. Despite Wright's own comments concerning Robinson in his prefatory statement to *The Green Wall,* the Robinson manner of writing—unadorned, lean, spare poems in which characterization is infinitely more important than description—is more evident in *Saint Judas* than in the initial book. "Paul," for example, owes a debt to Robinson's "The House on the Hill" for some of the phraseology, while the rhythms and situation of the poem bear general resemblances to those of Robinson. "Old Man Drunk" works with a sad, lonely man like Robinson's Eben Flood and Bewick Finzer, and the use of the word *futile* at the close of the poem seems to be borrowed from the conclusion of "Bewick Finzer":

> Face by face
> He grins to entertain, he fills my glass,
> Cold to the gestures of my vague *alas,*

9. Mills, *Contemporary American Poetry,* 204.
10. Crunk, "The Work of James Wright," 72.

> Gay as a futile god who cannot die
> Till daylight, when the barkeep says goodbye.
> ("Old Man Drunk")

> He comes unfailing for the loan
>   We give and then forget;
> He comes, and probably for years
>   Will he be coming yet,—
> Familiar as an old mistake,
>   And futile as regret.
> ("Bewick Finzer")

"The Refusal," in its direct, unadorned narrative set at a funeral and told from the collective "we" point of view, is similar in situation to any number of Robinson poems in which, as the case is in "The Refusal," the individual or individuals are condemned by others for not conforming to a specific behavioral pattern.

Saint Judas continues the studies of the outcasts and lonely begun in *The Green Wall*. For example, "A Note Left in Jimmy Leonard's Shack" concerns two old bums. But his poems of this ilk that deserve the most attention are those dealing with criminals. Crunk sees Wright in *Saint Judas* as possessed of two convictions: one, an awareness "that he is in some sense a criminal," and the other, "that he is somehow a man of good-will."[11] It is the former that engages our interest here, as does a remark Crunk makes in the early portion of his essay: "[Wright] has more respect for those who break laws than those who keep them."[12] There are three poems in the collection that focus on the criminal: "Saint Judas," the title poem, "American Twilights, 1957," dedicated to Caryl Chessman, and "At the Executed Murderer's Grave." In these poems, as Mills notes, Wright is obsessed with "themes of guilt and innocence, justice and punishment, moral right and hypocrisy."[13]

11. *Ibid.*, 57.
12. *Ibid.*, 54.
13. Mills, *Contemporary American Poetry*, 206.

"At the Executed Murderer's Grave" is divided into seven parts and, according to both Mills and Friedman, anticipates the manner Wright adopts in *The Branch Will Not Break;* they cite the subjectivity of the poem, the colloquial language and rhythms, the directness, and the regionalism as evidence.[14] Granting the above—the poem begins, "My name is James A. Wright, and I was born / Twenty-five miles from this infected grave, / In Martins Ferry, Ohio."—we are not convinced that the poem evidences enough of the qualities of the later poems to say unreservedly that it is a forerunner of the Emotive Imagination. Rather, the poem is more of a subjective confession of feelings Wright owns, and, at the same time, a self-indictment: He admits that he lies, that he croons his "tears at fifty cents per line," that he pities not the dead but the dying, that he pities himself, that he is an "unskilled criminal," and that he does not want to die.

In a 1962 anthology of British and American literature designed as a composition reader, James Wright is represented by two poems, one of which is "To the Ghost of a Kite," a poem that Wright has never published in any of his collections. Yet the poem is a brilliant accomplishment and represents one of his finest poems written strictly within the conventions. "To the Ghost of a Kite" consists of four stanzas of eight iambic pentameter lines rhymed *a b b a c d c d.* Traditional as the form of the poem assuredly is, the internal structuring is highly imaginative in the use of metaphor and symbol. The anthology, *Literature for Writing,* gives the poem's first publication as 1957, which means that "To the Ghost of a Kite" was available for publication in any of Wright's volumes. Several years ago the poet was asked why this poem, which we and other colleagues admire greatly, was not reprinted in any of his volumes. Surprised that the poem

14. *Ibid.,* 208; and Norman Friedman, "The Wesleyan Poets—III," *Chicago Review,* XIX (1967), 70.

was held in such repute, Wright replied, "I didn't think it was any good," and said that he would consider including it in *Collected Poems,* which was then in the making. To the volume's loss, he did not. Perhaps he held to his original estimation; perhaps the personal nature of the subject was too painful; perhaps echoes of "To the Ghost of a Kite" in his other already published poems were too clear. (There are similarities of phraseology and technique between the poem and "The Seasonless" and "The Horse" from *The Green Wall,* and "The Assignation" and "Evening" from *Saint Judas.*) Whatever his reasons, we are nonetheless convinced that "To the Ghost of a Kite" deserves serious attention and thus reproduce it below:

> Winter has wrecked the legend of your wings
> And thrown you down beside the cold garage.
> The silken gold that caught the air at large
> Wrinkles and fades among some rusted springs.
> There was a wind that sang below your breast,
> Astonished air blown seaward on your breath.
> That summer sound, lifted away and lost,
> Mutters around the corners of the earth.
>
> The season wrecks the legend of my child
> And blows his image of the summer down.
> He found the relic of your feathers blown
> To common birds, depleted and defiled.
> He was the child who ran below your flight,
> The dark hair flopping leaf-like over eyes,
> Who saw you leave your ballast for the light
> And shouted your escape across the skies.
>
> Back to the winter like a root he goes
> To nurture some great blossoms of your fire,
> To bring the year back and the pure desire
> For silken wings that never touch the grass.
> Winter has wrecked the legend of all wings.
> The sparrows scatter as I reach to hold
> One remnant of those proud, uncommon things:
> A warping stick turned yellow in the cold.

> Ghost of a dragon, tell me how to charm
> The spirit back to fill the body now.
> You vanished to the wind one year ago
> And left a broken string across my arm.
> Tell me the rune, the ballad, or the song
> To fling a rag upon a wand and build
> Some high magnificence to last as long
> As the clear vision of the summer child.

The speaker is a father who has lost his son; the title, imagery, and context suggest that the son died. The setting is delineated in the first two lines; the speaker sees the remnants of a kite next to a garage. This leads him to remember the soaring of a kite in summer, establishing early the contrast of winter to summer, the former standing for despair, loss, and death, and the latter for fullness of life, exhilaration, and joy. In addition, the opening stanza establishes the downward movement in imagery that is carried through the third stanza. The positive and exultant lines of the first stanza ("The silken gold that caught the air at large" and "There was a wind that sang below your breast, / Astonished air blown seaward on your breath") are tonally qualified by the negative lines immediately following in which loss and destruction are set forth. The use of the words *breast* and *breath* appear to serve as personification; but the speaker does use the kite throughout the poem on two elemental levels—as a man-made device and as a bird of the hawk family, a powerful predator. He also uses the kite and its ghost on several metaphoric levels, as well, as the poem progresses. Clearly, "To the Ghost of a Kite" is rich in what John Crowe Ransom calls "texture." The word *legend* in the first line, which is repeated in lines nine and twenty-one, introduces the concept of ritual on which the concluding stanza is predicated. The opening stanza, then, indicates the loss and suggests death, though the reader is unaware of the latter at this point in the poem.

The son is introduced in the opening line of the second stanza where the speaker recounts his son's delight in kite flying in the summer and his son's excitement as the kite string snapped. In addition, the fusion of kite as a device representative of adventure and kite as uncommon bird occurs in lines eleven and twelve. Just as death has wrecked the legend of the kite, so too has death ("The season") wrecked the legend of his child to the speaker-father, the first concrete indication in the poem that the boy died. The use of the words *image* and *relic* prepare us for the ritual ending of the poem.

Part of the thematic statement of the poem is contained in the opening four lines of the third stanza. Now winter assumes a different symbolic role: not death, but the state of dormancy necessary for rebirth. In this case, the speaker is not asking, nor does he ever ask in the poem, that the impossible be done, that his son be returned to life. Instead, he acknowledges that it is now time for him to bury deep in his mind the thoughts and memories he holds of his son so that there they may act as roots to provide some future growth for the father, in this instance to provide the father with the same fullness of life he experienced while his son was alive: "To bring the year back and the pure desire / For silken wings that never touch the grass." Thus the kite serves here the symbolic function of summer—fullness of life. But this act of consciously forgetting in the hope that renewal will occur is no easy task, as the father indicates when the reality of death strikes him: "Winter has wrecked the legend of all wings." Sparrows, the common birds contrasted to the hawk, scatter as the speaker-father reaches "to hold / One remnant of those proud, uncommon things," which, in the reality of winter's starkness, is only "A warping stick turned yellow in the cold." The stanza then ends with his having gone from the dream of hope to the desolation death exacts.

The final stanza is in the form of an invocation to the ghost of a kite, which was emblazoned with a dragon, to supply the spirit with something to replace the emptiness. The invocation itself, coupled with words like *rune* and *wand,* suggests some form of ancient magic, some ritualistic pattern that has existed since man first knew the need for spiritual replenishment. Interestingly, "Tell me the rune, the ballad, or the song" is, in fact, an historical survey of lyric poetry. The word *rune* has several meanings applicable to poetry: (1) rhymes or poetry in general; (2) Old Norse poetic lore; and (3) any poem that is mystic in nature. *Ballad* is self-explanatory, and *song,* of course, refers to a lyric poem. Now the main thematic thrust of "To the Ghost of a Kite" gains a clear perspective: the speaker-father wants to write a poem ("Some high magnificence") that not only will help to mitigate the loss he feels but will achieve a form of immortality and therefore will not be subject to death. It will be an immortality similar to "the clear vision of the summer child." In the poem proper, the speaker needs some form of magic to assist in the writing of the poem ("To fling a rag upon a wand"); this magic describes, as well, the construction of a kite, the kite then standing symbolically for "Some high magnificence." "To the Ghost of a Kite" is just that poem.

James Wright has built a remarkable poem of emotional depth, metaphoric and symbolic complexity and subtlety, and of structural and technical excellence. The death of a child is an emotional event that can be unparalleled in the life of a parent. Yet in this poem Wright's speaker-father does not use emotionally charged diction to convey his feelings; he lets metaphor, symbol, and the right rhythms carry the weight of the subject and attitude. To those like Crunk who fault Wright for his reliance on iambic pentameter, which Crunk believes needs "elaborate syntax" to sustain it and which necessarily hampers the natural voice, we offer "To the Ghost of a Kite" as self-sufficient evidence to the contrary.

The poem is also exemplary of Wright's early work. It treats the subject of death; its protagonist is lonely and alienated (from himself); and it works exclusively within the conventions of rhyme, meter, and stanzas.

In 1963, Wesleyan University Press, a major publishing house for the poets of the Emotive Imagination, issued James Wright's *The Branch Will Not Break,* the volume in which the manner of the Emotive Imagination is introduced and fulfilled and perhaps not coincidentally his most impressive single volume to date. The tone, subject matter, themes, and techniques are so altered from both *The Green Wall* and *Saint Judas* that the poems seem to come from another poet. Part I, Chapter 2, discusses Wright's readings in and translations of German and Spanish poetry, which obviously affected his decision to abandon the conventions in favor of new techniques, as did his personal association with Robert Bly. However, the task at hand is not to reiterate the why's, but rather to come to significant terms with the what's and how's of this new brand of poetry.

On the surface level, Wright's change can, in some measure, be detected by reading through the table of contents of *The Branch Will Not Break.* One comes across long, free-wheeling titles like "A Message Hidden in an Empty Wine Bottle That I Threw Into a Gully of Maple Trees One Night at an Indecent Hour," "Depressed by a Book of Bad Poetry, I Walk Toward an Unused Pasture and Invite the Insects to Join Me," and "From a Bus Window in Central Ohio, Just Before a Thunder Shower." More important is Wright's very extensive use of images from the natural world, images that often are metaphoric and work by means of the personification method. In "Beginning," Wright brilliantly creates an arcane atmosphere in which the speaker walks the middle ground between the human/animal world and the natural world of a wheat field. The poem opens with personifications and a metaphor—"The moon drops one or two feathers into the field. / The dark wheat listens"—and progresses by lines of irregular length through metaphors to an ending characteristic of poems of the Emotive Imagination in its subjective inwardness: "The wheat leans back toward its own darkness, / And I lean toward mine." "By a Lake in Minnesota" opens metaphorically:

> Upshore from the cloud—
> The slow whale of country twilight—
> The spume of light falls into valleys
> Full of roses—

then juxtaposes the above with an image of beavers, follows with a personification of the moon walking, "Hunting for hidden dolphins," and concludes with the poem turning inward to the speaker: "And downshore from the cloud, / I stand, waiting / For dark." It is not unusual for Wright to structure poems in *The Branch Will Not Break* by a series of observations of events, objects and situations in the external world, generally that of nature and usually by tropes, and then close the poem by having the speaker comment on his own situation. This is more or less the condition in "Lying in a Hammock at William Duffy's Farm in Pine Island, Minnesota," "The Jewel," "Fear Is What Quickens Me," "Trying to Pray," "Arriving in the Country Again," "Rain," and "Today I Was So Happy, So I Made This Poem." "Rain" is typical and brief enough to reproduce:

> It is the sinking of things.
>
> Flashlights drift over dark trees,
> Girls kneel,
> An owl's eyelids fall.
>
> The sad bones of my hands descend into a valley
> Of strange rocks.

The last two lines illustrate the muted shock effect at the end of the poem that is so often found in works of the Emotive Imagination.

"Lying in a Hammock at William Duffy's Farm in Pine Island, Minnesota," a frequently anthologized piece, is the most controversial Wright poem that follows the above pattern of observation through images and inward comment. For those in sympathy with the poets of the Emotive Imagination this poem is cited as a masterpiece. For others whose conception of poetry is more academic and who admire logical, discursive reasoning readily observable in poetry, "Lying in a Hammock" is no more than the ineffectual stringing together of illogically related images concluded by an unprepared-for personal comment:

> Over my head, I see the bronze butterfly,
> Asleep on the black trunk
> Blowing like a leaf in green shadow.
> Down the ravine behind the empty house,
> The cowbells follow one another
> Into the distances of the afternoon.
> To my right,
> In a field of sunlight between two pines,
> The droppings of last year's horses
> Blaze up into golden stones.
> I lean back, as the evening darkens and comes on.
> A chicken hawk floats over, looking for home.
> I have wasted my life.

Stephen Stepanchev, certainly not an academic critic who approves only the logically connected, nonetheless argues that the closing line of the poem does not work:

But it must be admitted that Wright does not always succeed in his new poems. His "deep image" does not always reverberate according to the plan because the occasion, the situation described in the poem, is too slight for the emotion that the poet says he is feeling: the details do not add up to the indicated experience. For example, in "Lying in a Hammock at William Duffy's Farm in Pine Island, Minnesota," Wright offers a number of rather pleasant descriptive details of an afternoon and evening and then concludes, without any sort of preparation: "I have wasted my life." This sort of observation, coming at the end of a poem, can have a tremendous impact if it represents a reversal of an established direction, but in this poem there is no real contrast and the line fails. [15]

15. Stepanchev, *American Poetry Since 1945*, 184–85.

On the other hand, both Norman Friedman and Crunk support the poem. Friedman says: "Some critics have said that this ending is neither prepared for nor supported by the rest of the poem, but I couldn't disagree more. The concluding statement is not only striking but apt.[16] While Crunk contends: "The mind here seems unnaturally, preternaturally, awake. It sees everything in delicate detail. The cowbells are like magic caravans; the dung of horses blazes up like alchemical stones. The poet leans back, goes deeper into himself. A glimpse of a chicken hawk reminds him that he has found nothing in his life to be sure of, that he has arrived nowhere, that he is still floating."[17]

When the reader comes to the last line, he knows the speaker has come to some realization while lying in the hammock, and that the realization is an important one, if not to the human condition as a whole, then to the speaker alone. Further, the reader senses that a loss in one form or another has been felt by the speaker and that this loss is related to what the speaker has been observing. In a public reading, Wright intones the concluding line as if the revelation comes as quite a shock. Alone this is not significant; but when it is taken in conjunction with the title and with the ordering devices behind the images, then meaning in a rational sense sharpens into focus, and the poem can be read as an organic, unified whole.

Value and belonging are the two concepts acting as ordering devices for the images in this poem. The butterfly "Blowing like a leaf in green shadow" is an attractive description delicately presented; its value is purely visual. Contrast this with a man lying in a hammock, a hammock that is, incidentally, not even his own. Since the butterfly is asleep, one can presume that it is "home." As the evening approaches the cows have a home toward which they are going, and the ringing of their bells creates presumably an attractive sound. The horse droppings have been transformed

16. Friedman, "The Wesleyan Poets—III," 71.
17. Crunk, "The Work of James Wright," 67.

by the late afternoon sun so that they resemble (indeed are, according to the metaphor) "golden stones." And, finally, the chicken hawk, a lowly predator, is described as floating, another attractive image; and it, in contrast to the man lying in someone else's hammock, is "looking for home"; it is engaged in the act of finding where it belongs. The final image, to which the others lead naturally, provokes "I have wasted my life"; the elements in and creatures of the natural world appear to the speaker in a more favorable light than he is able to view himself. The *wasted,* we can presume, refers to a self-appraisal upon his own lack of value and homelessness. As we have seen, Wright's speakers frequently are "homeless."

Although there are a few poems in *The Branch Will Not Break* concerned with death, the most impressive of which is "Miners," the poems, by and large, are noticeably free from the darkest preoccupations that mark most of the poems in his first two collections. Wright has never extricated himself completely from what Friedman calls "The dissatisfactions of the self" [18] but in *The Branch Will Not Break* there are even poems in which Wright expresses joy and exultation. The tone, however, is not always ecstatic. "I Was Afraid of Dying" is interesting since death has been such a major topic in his poetry. In this one he states very simply his fear in the title and in line two of this ten-line poem offers obliquely the reason he is no longer afraid: the patient tenacity of insects. "Milkweed" seems an important poem in any account and documentation of the tonal change in Wright's poetry. He tries to articulate this change in the final six lines of this twelve-line poem:

> Whatever it was I lost, whatever I wept for
> Was a wild, gentle thing, the small dark eyes
> Loving me in secret.
> It is here. At a touch of my hand,

---

18. Friedman, "The Wesleyan Poets—III," 70.

> The air fills with delicate creatures
> From the other world.

The phrase "At a touch of my hand" explicitly refers to the act of writing poetry, an act that allows Wright to create "delicate creatures / From the other world." The "other world" has two referents: (1) the natural world, which abounds in *The Branch Will Not Break;* and (2) the world of his imagination.

Wright's celebrations in this volume are most open in "Two Hangovers" ("Number Two: I Try to Waken and Greet the World Once Again"), "March," "Trying to Pray," "Today I Was So Happy, So I Made This Poem," and "A Blessing." In the first of these, from which the title of the collection is taken, the speaker sees a blue jay springing up and down on a branch and responds: "I laugh, as I see him abandon himself / To entire delight, for he knows as well as I do / That the branch will not break." The poem "March" describes a mother bear as "relaxed and beautiful"; and in "Trying to Pray," a poem squarely in the mode of the Emotive Imagination, the speaker exclaims, "There are good things in this world." Another Emotive Imagination poem, "Today I Was So Happy, So I Made This Poem," has the speaker, after watching a plump squirrel scampering "Across the roof of the corncrib" and the moon standing "up in the darkness," declare:

> And I see that it is impossible to die.
> Each moment of time is a mountain.
> An eagle rejoices in the oak trees of heaven,
> Crying
> *This is what I wanted.*

"A Blessing" is Wright's finest poem, not only in the manner of the Emotive Imagination, but in the canon of his poems to date. This judgment is not an isolated one, for the poem, since its 1963 appearance, has won the admiration of critics of every stance, anthologizers, teachers, students, and other poets. It is a poem very simply posited until the concluding three lines when the metaphoric leap approximates the condition of absolute joy. "A Blessing," as its title implies, is one of the most positive of Wright's poems, demonstrating the long distance from darkness he is capable of moving. Norman Friedman is right in his appraisal of the poem: "for sweetness, for joy, for precision, for rhythm, for eroticism, for structure, for surprise—for all these things, this poem is nearly perfect."[19]

"A Blessing" opens with delicate personification: "Just off the highway to Rochester, Minnesota, / Twilight bounds softly forth on the grass." Two Indian ponies whose eyes "Darken with kindness" capture the attention of the speaker and his friend, who cross the barbed wire and enter the pasture where the ponies "have been grazing all day." This act of recognition excites the ponies, who "ripple tensely" and who "can hardly contain their happiness" that the speaker and his friend are paying this visit. The speaker is drawn to the "slenderer one," who has come to him and nuzzled his left hand. The open, trusting, loving nature of the pony moves the speaker immensely, and he caresses "her long ear / That is delicate as the skin over a girl's wrist." The metaphor of the pony as a girl is quite obvious, and the poem is, as Friedman suggests, erotic. So touched and joyful is the speaker by his encounter with the ponies, particularly with the "slenderer one," that he exclaims in the closing lines of the poem: "Suddenly I realize / That if I stepped out of my body I would break / Into blossom." He nearly has the ability to transcend the empirical boundaries of the human condition and assume the larger (and more meaningful to him) properties inherent in all life. In fact, the speakers of a number of Wright's poems in *The Branch Will Not Break* seem to want to transcend the human into the purely natural, as indeed, James Dickey's speakers do, the difference being that Wright always recognizes that it is finally impossible to

19. *Ibid.*, 73.

do this; Dickey merely does it. Wright acknowledges his limits as a human; Dickey refuses to recognize that distinctions between the human, natural, and other animal states exist. Theodore Roethke, under whom Wright studied at the University of Washington, has, like Dickey, found it easier than has Wright to achieve this transcendence.

Despite the excellence attained in the use of images, personifications, and metaphoric leaps, all of which are evident in "A Blessing," there are poems in *The Branch Will Not Break* that simply do not succeed, poems in which one image is juxtaposed to another and then to another. Nothing else occurs. Three consecutive poems—"Two Spring Charms," "Spring Images," and "Arriving in the Country Again"—fall into this category. Crunk, who finds a number of faults to which Wright's poetry is subject, claims that the poet's use of images is sometimes perfunctory: "At times Wright deludes himself into believing he has a poem when he really hasn't anything."[20] In *The Distinctive Voice*, a 1966

---

20. Crunk, "The Work of James Wright," 76.

Crunk finds "softness" to be a flaw in the poetry of Wright: "In the early poetry, the softness is a vague, romantic mist that wraps everything. From the beginning his tendency has always been to make his experience more literary than it really is. For example, the girls tend to be dark, gentle, and romantic." (74)

Crunk continues his cataloguing of faults: "In *The Branch,* the poems about animals tend to be weak. The animals are often unreal. Evidently, what happens is that, tired of his own vision of the hostility of things, Wright assumes in animals a gentleness that is not there. Poems like 'Trying to Pray,' 'To the Evening Star,' and 'Beginning' are weak in that way." (75)

Crunk finds, too, that the "grammar also tends to be too repetitive," explaining that "in *The Branch,* there are too many 'of' phrases: inhuman fire of jewels, hallways of a diamond, pillows of the sea, happiness of small winds, oak trees of heaven, waters of air, shores of melting snow, etc." (75) Crunk then distinguishes between the kinds of "of" phrases that Wright so frequently employs: one, the purely descriptive; two, the metaphorical, a word Crunk will not mention but which is nonetheless the only one to describe accurately his explanation of the second kind of "of" phrase: "When a man says 'ruins of the sun' he is imagining a substance that is neither ruins nor sun, but some third substance, which has never existed before, created by the words. Other examples are 'daylight of the body,' 'black waters of the suburbs,' 'heaven of my skull.' These constructions cannot be rephrased. They are a kind of vision, rather than a description. Nevertheless, the reader has the feeling there are too many 'of's.'" (76)

Crunk also finds in Wright's work a "tendency to evade practical problems—that is anthology, Louis Simpson warns against the indiscriminate use of images: "But Surrealist poets have often failed to see that mere images, however new, are not enough. Their images are drawn from a deeper level, the subconscious. But they are merely projected on a screen, where they remain motionless. The deepest image, if it does not move, is only an object. And it's no use multiplying images . . . nothing happens."[21] Robert Bly is also guilty on the same score for which he condemns Wright and that Simpson articulates above.

There are additional poems in *The Branch Will Not Break* that recommend themselves to the serious reader for diverse reasons: "Miners," for its oblique but nonetheless compelling study in death; "Eisenhower's Visit to Franco, 1959," for a political poem devoid of the strenuous diction and attitudes so common to poems of this kind and for its images ("a triumph in the simple use of images");[22] "In Memory of a Spanish Poet," for its treatment of Miguel Hernández and for its muted ending by means of personification; "A Prayer to Escape from the Market Place," for Wright's belief in a superiority the natural world holds over commercialism, including the literary market place; "Twilights," for a successful poem in the fashion of the Emotive Imagination; and "Fear Is What Quickens Me," for its seeming irrationality of disconnected images that indeed possess unity and coherence and for its abrupt but appropriate conclusion.

---

problems requiring action. The way he does it is by escalating them into terms appropriate to Armageddon or the Apocalypse." (76)

Finally: "The most general fault, then, is a tendency not to bite deeply enough into hard material, but to slide over it. Wright's powerful intelligence is always awake during the poem chewing on the problem of making a *poem*, but it does not always stay on the *subject*." (77) This is a criticism on which we are in general agreement with Crunk. Louis Simpson's earlier poems are subject to the same charge. But in poems since 1959, Simpson has overcome this to the extent that he penetrates often too deeply for some readers.

21. William J. Martz, *The Distinctive Voice: Twentieth-Century American Poetry* (Glenview, Ill.: Scott, Foresman & Company, 1966), 247.

22. Crunk, "The Work of James Wright," 73.

One poem, "Autumn Begins in Martins Ferry, Ohio," stands alone in *The Branch Will Not Break*. It is true, certainly, that its use of place-names and its setting in the American Midwest align it with other poems in the collection, as well as with other poems by the writers of the Emotive Imagination. But it activates a series of interesting contrasts predicated on the citizens of Martins Ferry, Ohio, Wright's home town, that is absent in other poems in *The Branch Will Not Break*. It contrasts not only youth and age, but heroes and ordinary human beings, by using the setting of a high school football game in the local stadium. The fathers of the players feel inadequate because their sons have promises to fulfill, futures ahead of them; the youths are now community heroes, heroes of the tribe, while their fathers are depicted as "nursing long beers" or as working at menial jobs in the steel mills of the area. And the fathers, drinking or working, are "Dreaming of heroes"; these dreams may be glorified memories as well, since they may relate to the status the fathers once held as football heroes themselves. From this there is the suggestion that the futures of the current community heroes may be as bleak as the present time assuredly is for the fathers.

The second stanza of this brief, three-stanza poem documents the fathers' feelings of inadequacy through sexual imagery: "All the proud fathers are ashamed to go home. / Their women cluck like starved pullets, / Dying for love." When compared to their sons, the fathers must seem inferior, yet their wives want the sexual gratification their husbands feel they cannot adequately provide. The use of the word *pullets,* other than the obvious hen reference, may bear some relationship to *poule,* a slang French word for prostitute, thus adding another dimension to the sexual imagery. The final stanza demonstrates the way in which the men compensate: by their transferal to the dramatic, forceful *action* of their sons on the football field. In addition, the fathers are probably reliving the times they were the heroes:

Therefore,
Their sons grow suicidally beautiful
At the beginning of October,
And gallop terribly against each other's bodies.

The poetry of James Wright and Robert Bly is similar stylistically; that is, the poems in Wright's *The Branch Will Not Break*
resemble Bly's in *Silence in the Snowy Fields,* and to a lesser degree
there are likenesses between their poems from the mid–1960s on.
Bly's influence on Wright has been apparent in the latter's poems
from the end of the 1950s. But the similarities between Wright
and both Louis Simpson and William Stafford, other than in their
allegiances to the methods of the Emotive Imagination, are not
immediately noticeable. True, Wright, Stafford, and Simpson
write about their fathers in compelling poems; true, their subjects are primarily rural rather than urban; and true, Wright and
Stafford use place-names and are "regional" writers. And there
are several poems in *The Branch Will Not Break* in which close
parallels with poems by Simpson and Stafford exist. Take, for
instance, these excerpts from Simpson's "Lines Written Near
San Francisco" and Wright's "Stages on a Journey Westward":

Every night, at the end of America
We taste our wine, looking at the Pacific.
How sad it is, the end of America!
. . . .
Out there on the Pacific
There's no America but the Marines.
                    (Simpson)

At the bottom of the cliff
America is over and done with.
America,
Plunged into the dark furrows
Of the sea again.
                    (Wright)

Or take these from Simpson's "The Redwoods" and Wright's "Two Hangovers":

> We [the redwoods] stand at the Pacific
> like great unmarried girls,
> (Simpson)

> Locusts and poplars change to unmarried women.
> (Wright)

Three lines from Wright's "To the Evening Star: Central Minnesota" perhaps owe a debt to the concluding stanza of Stafford's "West of Your City":

> West of this wide plain
> Animals wilder than ours
> Come down from the green mountains in the darkness.
> (Wright)

> *Cocked in that land tactile as leaves*
> *wild things wait crouched in these valleys*
> *west of your city outside your lives*
> *in the ultimate wind, the whole land's wave.*
> *Come west and see; touch these leaves.*
> (Stafford)

Apparently the period from 1959 to 1963, when Wright was composing the poems to be included in *The Branch Will Not Break,* was an interlude in which the newness of his altered style had some measurable effect on the subject and tones of the poems. For in the poems of his next collection, *Shall We Gather at the River* (1968), he returns to the subjects that weighted down *The Green Wall* and *Saint Judas*—death, loneliness, isolation of the self—and to the alienated, lost, forgotten characters who abound in his first two collections and who are absent from *The Branch Will Not Break.* [23]

---

23. Death and the subsequent return to life, often but not always in the guise of a ghost, has been a subject Wright has worked with since *The Green Wall:* "The Angel" and

The prefatory poem to the book, "A Christmas Greeting," written in heroic couplets except for the concluding line, is addressed to Charlie, a man who committed suicide. The poem, which is a meditation on death ("I'm afraid to die, / It hurts to die, although the lucky do."), establishes the tone of the entire collection, one of gloom, despair, and morbid introspection. [24] In addition, his poems concerning the self are perhaps even more intense than those in the preceding collections. For example, in "Before a Cashier's Window in a Department Store," a five-part poem in which desolation and personal despair are total, the impoverished, depressed speaker announces: "I am the dark. I am the dark / Bone I was born to be." And in "Speak," which, along with "For the Marsh's Birthday," is written within prosodic conventions, the speaker declares:

> I have gone forward with
> Some, a few lonely some.
> They have fallen to death.
> I die with them.

A few more instances of Wright's concern with the morbid aspects of self will suffice to provide the reader with an overview, tonally and thematically, of *Shall We Gather at the River,* a volume that represents a marked dropping off for Wright. At the outset of "The River Down Home," in which the alienated of society are subjects, the speaker cites a death by drowning, a means of death

---

"The Assignation" from that volume; "The Ghost" and "The Alarm" from *Saint Judas;* and "The Life," "To the Muse," and "In Response to a Rumor that the Oldest Whorehouse in Wheeling, West Virginia, Has Been Condemned" from *Shall We Gather at the River.* In the last, one of the stronger poems in the collection, Wright interjects ironic humor, clearly an unusual device for him.

24. *Shall We Gather at the River* is addressed to Jenny. "Speak" concerns Jenny, who "Has broken her spare beauty / In a whorehouse old." Jenny is also addressed in "To the Muse"; black prostitutes are alluded to in "The Minneapolis Poem"; the word *cathouses* appears in "The River Down Home"; and the title "In Response to a Rumor that the Oldest Whorehouse in Wheeling, West Virginia, Has Been Condemned" speaks to the subject.

frequently employed by Wright; and following this come lines exemplifying Wright's state of depression in this book:

> Outside my window, now, Minneapolis
> Drowns, dark.
> It is dark.
> I have no life.

"To the Muse" contains this open, personal, prosy indictment: "I wish to God I had made this world, this scurvy / And disastrous place." Finally, from "Listening to the Mourners," comes this: "The grief that I hear is my life somewhere."

William Stafford has written poems on the subject of the American Indian from the beginning of his career. Simpson, in *At the End of the Open Road,* the New Poems division of his *Selected Poems* (1965), and in *Adventures of the Letter I* (1971), demonstrates that the American Indian is becoming a subject of significant interest to him. Simpson records the following observations in *North of Jamaica,* his autobiography. The "we" of the first sentence includes Bly, Wright, and some unidentified writers:

At this time we were writing Indian Poems. The Indian was being taken up again as a symbol. It was nostalgia, and something more: in their search for a way of life to identify with, poets were turning to an idea of the dark, suppressed American. We talked, I remember, about the "inner life." Some day someone will take the poems about Indians written by men as different as Bly and Snyder and discover what they were driving at. The Indian, I have no doubt, was as foolish as the white man, and the people who settled Kentucky would have wondered at our sympathy for howling savages. History and poetry are far apart; poems about Indians were a fantasy of sophisticated twentieth-century people who were trying to find ways out of the materialism that was everywhere around them. [25]

Shall We Gather at the River includes a sequence of poems— "Inscription for the Tank," "In Terror of Hospital Bills," and "I

---

25. Louis Simpson, *North of Jamaica* (New York: Harper & Row, 1972), 241–42.

Am a Sioux Brave, He Said in Minneapolis"—in which Wright treats the subject. Although "Inscription for the Tank" nowhere mentions Indians as such, we can infer on the basis of evidence linking the poem to "In Terror of Hospital Bills" that the inscription, "My life was never so precious / To me as now," was scrawled on the wall of the drunk tank by the Sioux speaker of "In Terror of Hospital Bills," who utters the phrase also in that poem. In the latter, a metaphorically structured poem, the Sioux is frightened, alone, and nearly destitute. In other words, he is a typical Wright protagonist of *Shall We Gather at the River*. The same Sioux is the subject of the final poem of the sequence, a poem employing the Emotive Imagination method, particularly in the last five lines:

> The black caterpillar
> Crawls out, what with one thing
> And another, across
> The wet road.
> How lonely the dead must be.

The sentence ending the poem provides a muted shock as the speaker leaps from the image of the caterpillar to his statement, a rather odd one, of death.

The techniques of the Emotive Imagination are noticeably visible in a number of poems in this volume. There are some failures, such as "Living by the Red River" and "To Flood Stage Again," in which little more is achieved than the juxtaposing of images followed by personal statements that strike the reader as artificial. But there are successes, too, notably "Late November in a Field," "Listening to the Mourners," "Youth," "The Life," "The Small Blue Heron," "To the Poets in New York," and "Poems to a Brown Cricket." "To the Poets in New York," addressed probably to the Frank O'Hara group, is a calm, metaphorically structured poem that is compassionate without being so overtly tragic that the reader is told how to respond. *Shall We*

Gather at the River would be a stronger volume if it had more poems of this kind to balance those in which the personal despair is blatantly confessional.

In 1971, Wesleyan University Press published James Wright's *Collected Poems,* the Pulitzer selection for 1972. The *Collected Poems* contains all the poems included in the four previously published volumes of original poetry, two prefatory poems ("The Quest" and "Sitting in a Small Screenhouse on a Summer Morning"), about twenty pages of translations,[26] and thirty-one new poems. Surprisingly, the New Poems division contains five poems written in the formal conventions: "So She Said," "Humming a Tune for an Old Lady in West Virginia," "To a Dead Drunk," "Written in a Copy of Swift's Poems, for Wayne Burns," and "The Offense." But on reflection perhaps this is not so surprising since half the poems deal with the same early subjects of death and alienation. Even though Wright is traditional in the above poems, his style in others evinces a certain loosening or dropping off into prose not found in the previous collections. He uses the word *hell* as a curse with some regularity in these poems, which may serve as an index of this new stance of increased informality. Frankly, much of the excellent sense of rhythm that distinguishes the 1963 volume and is somewhat lacking in the 1968 one is even less evident in the New Poems. In addition, and corollary with the "new" looseness, Wright has become more disgusted in his attitude toward the human condition, exemplified in this excerpt from "A Secret Gratitude":

> Man's heart is the rotten yolk of a blacksnake egg
> Corroding, as it is just born, in a pile of dead
> Horse dung.
> I have no use for the human creature.

26. The translations are from the Spanish of Juan Ramón Jiménez, Jorge Guillén, Pablo Neruda, César Vallejo, and Pedro Salinas; and from the German of Georg Trakl and Goethe.

> He subtly extracts pain awake in his own kind.
> I am born one, out of an accidental hump of chemistry.
> I have no use.

This attitude coupled with the personal despair tends, indeed, to make Wright something of a confessional poet, though critics, for the most part, have rarely grouped him with, say, Anne Sexton and Sylvia Plath.

Other poems in the New Poems section recall some of Wright's earlier topics: Love ("The Idea of the Good," "Moon," "To Harvey, Who Traced the Circulation"); the American Indian ("A Centenary Ode: Inscribed to Little Crow, Leader of the Sioux Rebellion in Minnesota, 1862"); and, naturally, death, despair, and alienation, of which there are too many to list. There is a protest poem, too ("A Mad Fight Song for William S. Carpenter, 1966"), and two poems ("Many of Our Waters: Variations on a Poem by a Black Child" and "A Moral Poem Freely Accepted from Sappho") concerning the writing of poetry. The former one on poetry is Wright's longest poem to date and was delivered as the Phi Beta Kappa poem, College of William and Mary, on December 5, 1969. Its situation is described in the prose introduction in Part 1 of this seven-part poem.[27] The concluding stanzas are important enough to reproduce since Wright's apparently

27. The prose introduction concerns Garnie Braxton, the black child of the title and the subject of "A Poem by Garnie Braxton." Both the prose and the brief poem are reproduced below:

from my journal, March 8, 1969: Garnie's whisper to me, while we were watching a construction operation near Radio City. The operation had reached that early stage at which the workmen had dug extremely deep into the intended foundation of the building, obviously therefore to be a new skyscraper. As Garnie watched the working men, they were far below, and, to his eyes, as to mine, they appeared very small. About a third of them were Negroes. And this is exactly what he whispered to me. It has to, and it can—only it can—speak for itself.

*   *   *   *

"Garnie, I wish I was a seagull."

"Yeah, me too.
And when you want to get warm
All you got to do

new attitude toward poetry is stated along with one of his attitudes toward the human condition:

> All this time I've been slicking into my own words
> The beautiful language of my friends.
> I have to use my own, now.
> That's why this scattering poem sounds the way it does.
> You're my brother at last,
> And I don't have anything
> Except my brother
> And many of our waters in our native country,
> When they break.
> And when they break,
> They break in a woman's body,
> They break in your man's heart,
> And they break in mine:
>
> Pity so old and alone, it is not alone, yours, or mine,
> The pity of rivers and children, the pity of brothers, the pity
> Of our country, which is our lives.

The "pity" of which he speaks is tonally quite different from
the indictment he leveled at the human race in the excerpt quoted
earlier from "A Secret Gratitude." In fact, there is quite a var-
iance of tones in the New Poems. The final poem of the section
concludes with this: "There must be something very beautiful in
my body, / I am so happy."

There are strong indications in the New Poems, despite those
pieces written in the conventions, that Wright in the late 1960s
and early 1970s is still committed to the techniques of the Emotive Imagination. Though his use of the personification method is
less visible, he retains the device of metaphoric leaps to structure
many of the poems. "Moon," an overtly emotional poem about
Jenny, concludes with a transformation similar in kind to that
which takes place at the end of "A Blessing":

> Is put on feathers
> And fly away to the south.
> I been there once."

> And I love you,
> Sky full of laurels and arrows,
> White shadow of cities where the scars
> Of forgotten swans
> Waken into feathers
> And new leaves.

"Small Frogs Killed on the Highway," the most exemplary in manner of the Emotive Imagination, posits a moral: that life lived to the fullest, even if foreseeable death is a constant threat, is the only meaningful way to exist. The speaker argues at the outset that he "would leap too / Into the light [car headlights]" if he had the chance. The world on the other side of the road is "everything, the wet green stalk of the field." It is the instant of heightened life just before death that makes leaping across the road at night worth the risk: "many / Of the dead are alive forever in the split second" of the auto headlights. This small poem ends with a meditation on the tadpoles, who, once they are able to see, must make their decisions. Obviously, Wright is drawing a parallel between frogs and people:

> Across the road, tadpoles are dancing
> On the quarter thumbnail
> Of the moon. They can't see,
> Not yet. [28]

In 1973, two years after *Collected Poems,* Farrar, Straus and Giroux published Wright's *Two Citizens,* for whose dust jacket Wright has written:

Two Citizens is an expression of my patriotism, of my love and discovery of my native place. I never knew or loved my America so well, and I begin the book with a savage attack upon it. Then I discovered it. It took the shape of a beautiful woman who loved me and who led me through

---

28. Compare these lines with the conclusion of "I Am a Sioux Brave, He Said in Minneapolis," quoted in the text.

France and Italy. I discovered my America there. That is why this is most of all a book of love poems. The two citizens are Annie and I.

It is not surprising, then, that in these thirty-two poems the word *love* and its variations (*loved, lovers, lovely, lovelier*) appear in all but four of the poems. Love is employed not only to express his feeling for his wife, Annie, to whom the volume is dedicated along with their friend Rae Tufts; it is used as well as a means by which Wright has been able to effect a reconciliation with himself and his country. Signs of such reconciliation are withheld, however, until the "savage attack upon [America]" has been, by and large, concluded. Poems found early in the collection (e.g., "Ars Poetica: Some Recent Criticism," "The Last Drunk," "The Young Good Man," "Ohio Valley Swains") take us back, in varying degrees of despondency and bitterness, to the tonal urgencies of *Shall We Gather at the River* and the New Poems division of *Collected Poems,* and to Wright's life as a child in Ohio as well as to some earlier adult experiences.

In some of these poems America is indeed indicted, as in these excerpts from "Ars Poetica: Some Recent Criticism" and "Son of Judas":

> I don't believe in your god.
> I don't believe my Aunt Agnes is a saint.
> I don't believe the little boys
> Who stoned the poor
> Son of a bitch goat
> Are charming Tom Sawyers.
>
> I have bought your world.
> I don't want it.
> And I don't want all your money
> I got sucked into making
> Either.

But the opening poems belie the significant change evident in most of the poems in *Two Citizens*. Wright's preoccupation with the dark—his depression and despair—has given way to a joy of sorts, not the freedom he experienced when discovering harmony with the natural world (*The Branch Will Not Break*), but an exhilaration occasioned by love.[29]

Although "Afternoon and Evening at Ohrid," the seventh poem in the collection, is not about America, which, as Wright says, is the subject of the opening pieces, it is the first poem in *Two Citizens* in which we encounter Wright as a man markedly changed from what we had come to expect since the mid-1960s. Even though she is not mentioned by name, Annie must be the catalytic agent responsible for the transformation revealed in "I Wish I May Never Hear of the United States Again," which is set in Yugoslavia and which serves as the fulcrum poem on the subject of America in the volume. The poet and Annie are unable to speak or understand Serbo-Croatian; and the poet is nearly reduced to silence by the awareness of his own limitations, and, at the same time, by the serenity and loveliness of the images of people and the natural world surrounding Annie and him. What Wright does say, or try to say, in this oddly titled poem is that in Europe, distanced from America and with Annie as a guide, he is learning to reinterpret his native land.

This discovery may be further illustrated. In "Paul"[30] Wright acknowledges America to be "That brutal and savage place whom I still love," which should be contrasted with the opening lines of the collection: "I loved my country, / When I was a little boy." The inference legitimately drawn is that Wright in "Ars Poetica: Some Recent Criticism" had outgrown his love for America; yet this love is reaffirmed a few poems later in the

29. In "A Poem of Towers," for instance, the speaker, who is Wright as he is throughout *Two Citizens,* identifies with the "old men" as he has since *The Green Wall,* and with the familiar lost, forgotten, and alienated of our society; but in this poem he declares: "I wonder about them, / And how they became / So happy." The poem is a testament to the effect of Annie on the poet.

30. "Paul" is also the title of a poem in *Saint Judas;* the same character is apparently involved in both poems.

volume, another testimonial to the transformational role of Annie.

Other poems in which Wright views America (and himself) from an altered perspective include "A Poem of Towers," "Names Scarred at the Entrance to Chartres," "She's Awake," and "To the Creature of the Creation." Another of his poems involving America might serve to dissuade us from arguing the presence of a totally regenerate Wright in his attitude toward his country. In "To You, Out There (Mars? Jupiter?)," the speaker facetiously considers what the Martians, or whatever, would observe were they to sight their lenses on New York's theater district, the vision including people

> . . . standing for hours in a line, huddling
> Alone in the griped cold, hopelessly longing
> To pray to someone whose name
> Is Streisand.

In a series of exorbitant images that follow, the speaker describes the Earth's (and America's) sad concerns. Yet the poem is predicated on such fantasy that its indictment is nearly lost, or is, at the least, considerably softened.

Several of the poems in *Two Citizens* address the need of the poet to find new words to identify, define, and express perceptions that might have been known and felt before but not revealed because of the inadequacy of the poet or of the language in which he felt imprisoned. Since *Two Citizens* represents a new direction for Wright, we are not surprised but rather expect that the poems express the difficulties he encountered in working with a language that had become so familiar to him. He tries to tell Annie in "Voices Between Waking and Sleeping in the Mountains" of a childhood experience in Ohio, but fails to say it adequately: "If only I knew how to tell you. / Some day I may know how." It is natural to conjoin Annie in this struggle with language, since she is purportedly responsible for the Wright projected in these poems. Wright states in "To the Creature of the Creation" and elsewhere that it is hard to articulate both newly discovered and older emotions, for his language is a confining one: "No, I ain't much. / The one tongue I can write in / Is my Ohioan."

But by the end of *Two Citizens,* James Wright has been able to achieve an inner calm, a confidence inspired by Annie that nearly obliges the poet to accept himself, his Ohio past, and to fail the best way he can in the language he knows the best. The volume concludes with these lines from "To the Creature of the Creation":

> Some day I have to die,
> As everyone must do
> Alone, alone, alone,
> Peaceful as peaceful stone.
> You are the earth's body.
> I will die on the wing.
> To me, you are everything
> That matters, chickadee.
> You live so much in me.
> Chickadees sing in the snow.
> I will die on the wing,
> I love you so.

It is significant, too, that in this acceptance of death Wright reverts to the conventions of rhyme and an irregular metrical pattern, though the style is obviously mannered.

Two Citizens is Wright's most personal volume to date. "In Memory of Charles Coffin," "At the Grave," "Voices Between Sleeping and Waking in the Mountains," "The Art of the Fugue: A Prayer," "The Snail's Road," "She's Awake," and "To the Creature of the Creation"—some of which have already been cited in one context or another—stand out as personal statements. In the first two, which concern one of Wright's former teachers, the poet expresses unabashed sentiment, as in these excerpts taken respectively from the poems: "My loving teacher, whom I love, / It is almost too late to live"; "The essay wasn't all that good, but you loved it, / And you loved me." The following address to Annie, which comes from "Voices Between Sleeping and Waking in the Mountains," is exemplary of the prosiness to which Wright is subject when he succumbs to the openly personal: "Annie, it has taken me a long time to live. / And to take a long time to live is to take a long time / To understand that your life is your own life." The looseness that naturally accompanies such verbosity is also a holdover from the New Poems division of *Collected Poems*.

Apparently the James Wright of *Two Citizens* accepts into his poetry any strongly felt emotions, so long as they serve to illuminate his transformation. We believe Wright could have profited by exercising his editorial prerogative; many of these poems demonstrate emotion sentimentally and thus are ineffectual. For the personal poem to succeed as more than merely a recording of emotion, it needs to engage the reader's sensibilities. It is not enough just to tell, as Wright has elected to do in too many of these poems, what he feels and has experienced. One of the lasting values of the Emotive Imagination, when it is effectively used, is the ability to make the reader respond to the sensations and thoughts the poet is attempting to convey through images. We have observed that, as Bly, Wright, and Simpson continue to write, they are relying more on direct expression of emotion and less on the techniques of the Emotive Imagination that distinguished them from their contemporaries in the 1960s. The result is that their poetry is tending to be at times indistinguishable from prose. (Although Stafford's method depends in part on using the prose statement, he does not tell his readers what the emotion is.)

Wright has not yet abandoned his allegiance to the Emotive Imagination. In over a quarter of the poems in *Two Citizens*, he uses it with varying degrees of accomplishment—from "Hotel Lenox," a somewhat contrived exercise in which Wright is content to reel off one image after another, to "The Old WPA Swimming Pool in Martins Ferry, Ohio," an interesting, mildly nostalgic piece. To the boy of the poem, the pool can be contrasted only to the other gouges in the earth he knew—graves. The poem ends with the image of a little girl the boy saw when he "rose from that water," whose face was "thin and haunted" and who whispered to him to "Take care now, / Be patient, and live." In what is a familiar method in *Two Citizens,* the poem concludes: "I have loved you all this time, / And didn't even know / I am alive." It is interesting to consider the girl as an embodiment of America, whose discovery in this context was withheld to the poet until his European trip with Annie.

In "Voices Between Waking and Sleeping in the Mountains," the poet recounts a time in Martins Ferry when he sat in a sycamore tree and, embracing the tree, felt that he was out of himself and into a new life. The sycamore, in good Emotive Imagination fashion, is likened to a woman, as it also is in "Son of Judas"; the sensation remembered by the poet is indistinguishable, as he relates it, from love and the purely sexual. In "Son of Judas" the sycamore tree is the physical location where the poet first experienced a sexual awakening: "I rose out of my body so high into / That sycamore tree that it became / The only tree that ever loved me."

"At the Grave" closes in a manner appropriate to the Emotive Imagination:

> And blessed your thorned face,
> Your shragged November,
> Your leaf,
> Lost.

The metaphoric leaps in this excerpt from "Afternoon and Evening at Ohrid" would have qualified for inclusion ten years earlier in *The Branch Will Not Break:*

> I already know
> My friends the spiders. They are mountains.
> Every spider in America is the shadow
> Of a beautiful woman.

It is not difficult to find other instances to substantiate the claim that Wright's work still embodies the principles of the Emotive

Imagination, but we acknowledge, nonetheless, that Wright and the Emotive Imagination have been in a gradual process of disengaging since 1963.

In "Many of Our Waters: Variations on a Poem by a Black Child" (New Poems division of *Collected Poems*), Wright admits that he has been "slicking into . . . / The beautiful language of my friends" [Bly? Duffy?] and therefore now must use his own language. From signs in the 1971 collection, we could expect to materialize the prosy, confessional, and less emotively structured poetry of *Two Citizens*. What we could not have foreseen, however, was the direction Wright chose to pursue in his latest volume. Perhaps in the future, we can hope Wright will explore other new areas of inquiry. (Love, as such, is not a new subject for Wright, but his treatment of it as personally regenerative assuredly is in *Two Citizens*.) To be certain, Wright is not a poet whose subject interests can yet be called heterogeneous, yet the changed perceptions of self, the past, and America augur well for the prospect of Wright's challenging new concerns. Wright is still, we hasten to add, broader in his subject matter than Robert Bly. Louis Simpson, to whom the following chapter is devoted, has worked with some topics regularly; and, like Wright, he adopted the Emotive Imagination about 1959.[31] Simpson, however, has been continually alert to new subjects and new perceptions into these subjects.

---

31. In *North of Jamaica*, Louis Simpson alludes to a time, presumably in the late 1950s, when James Wright and he, along with others, were guests at Robert Bly's farm in Madison, Minnesota: "James Wright read one of his new poems. He had begun, like so many others, with poems that were traditional. His early poems had been filled with echoes of E. A. Robinson. . . . His new poems were different; you could have described the changes in American poetry in recent years just by listing the differences between Wright's first book and his new manuscript [*The Branch Will Not Break*]." Simpson then quotes "Autumn Begins in Martins Ferry, Ohio" as illustrative of the differences. *North of Jamaica*, 240–41.

3 Louis Simpson

SINCE 1949, Louis Simpson has published six volumes of poetry, one of which, *At the End of the Open Road* (1963), was awarded the Pulitzer Prize. He has also put together a poetry reader, *Introduction to Poetry* (1967 and 1972); written critical and personal essays; edited with Donald Hall and Robert Pack *New Poets of England and America* (1957); translated a number of pieces from French to English, including Guillaume Apollinaire's *The Breasts of Tiresias;* written a full-length critical work, *James Hogg: A Critical Study* (1962); published a fine novel, *Riverside Drive* (1962); and published his autobiography, *North of Jamaica* (1972).[1] Although Simpson's creative work extends beyond poetry, it is that genre that makes up the subject of this chapter, which first examines Simpson's techniques and then the range of subjects he has challenged in the past thirty years.

Like James Wright, Simpson began his career in poetry by adhering closely to the traditional forms of rhyme, meter, and regularized stanzas; then toward the end of the 1950s and begin-

1. For a complete treatment of Simpson's poetry and novel, see Ronald Moran, *Louis Simpson* (New York: Twayne Publishers, Inc., 1972); this book provides detailed explications of many poems discussed in this chapter. For a discussion of Simpson's criticism, see Ronald Moran, "Louis Simpson: The Absence of Criticism and the Presence of Poetry," *The Far Point,* I (Fall/Winter, 1968), 60–66.

ning of the 1960s, Simpson departed from the restrictions that commitments to formal elements demanded and adopted the methods of the Emotive Imagination. A number of Simpson's earlier poems—those from *The Arrivistes* (1949), *Good News of Death and Other Poems* (1955), and *A Dream of Governors* (1959)—represent excellent achievements in formally oriented poetry.

Simpson spent 1948/49 in Paris, during which time he collected many of his lyrics and two verse plays he had written between 1940 and 1949 into his first volume, *The Arrivistes,* printed at his own cost and bearing the imprint of the Fine Editions Press in New York. One could characterize the tone of these lyrics as witty and ironic. Part of the wit comes from his use of inversions and other archaic devices. In some of these poems, Simpson resembles Elizabethan and Cavalier song makers.[2] Other poems, such as "Arm in Arm" and "Carentan O Carentan," two very serious war poems, are ballad-like, with alternating iambic tetrameter and trimeter lines and a basic *a b a b* rhyme scheme, the result of which is a rather flip, sing-song rhythm that paradoxically underscores and masquerades the sober subject matter.

"Carentan O Carentan," the finest accomplishment in *The Arrivistes,* has been reprinted by Simpson in both *A Dream of Governors* and *Selected Poems* (1965), just as the sonnet "Summer Storm" has been. "A Witty War," rewritten as "The Custom of the World" and reprinted in both the later volumes, is typical of the early Simpson. Though in its original version "A Witty War" lacks substance, this love poem is clever and technically sound. The quality of writing in the second version is quite superior to the first; Simpson eliminates the repartee of wit, from

2. Writing in the February 19, 1950, number of the *New York Times Book Review,* Milton Cane says "Invitation to a Quiet Life" succeeds "in maintaining within its frame a delightful unity of tone and diction which is neither wholly seventeenth nor wholly twentieth century"; it is, he continues, "an ironic rewriting of a pastoral by Andrew Marvell or Robert Herrick."

which the original title is taken, sharpens his images, and re-
works several of the lines, eliminating passages that seemed
rhythmically awkward.

The only other poem Simpson felt should be preserved from
The Arrivistes, which was printed in a limited edition, is a fine
love lyric, "Song: 'Rough Winds Do Shake the Darling Buds of
May.' " Reprinted in both *A Dream of Governors* and *Selected
Poems,* the poem carries the abbreviated title "Rough Winds Do
Shake" in the former, while the full title is restored in the latter.
This poem has undergone but one change in the reprintings: the
inclusion of a comma. The poem is a successful experiment in the
topographical arrangement of lines; it concerns a sexually excita-
ble girl who is

> sixteen
> > and her young lust
>
> Is like a thorn
> > hard thorn
> > > among the pink
>
> Of her soft nest.

In other poems, such as the war pieces "Roll" and "Resistance," Simpson is deliberately rough in his metrics; and in
"Room and Board," roughly a sonnet, he dispenses with the wit
and irony that mark most of the poems from his original collection:

> The curtained windows of New York
> Conceal her secrets. Walls of stone
> Muffle the clatter of the fork.
> Tomorrow we shall see the bone.
>
> In silence we construct a sect . . .
> Each of us, comrades, has his own.
> Poems that will not take effect,
> Pictures that never will be known.
>
> The landlord wipes his mouth of pork,
> Pauses to eavesdrop, disconnects
> The water and the telephone;

> And Death's unmarried daughter crawls
> Along the thin lath of the walls
> And knocks, because we live alone.

In "Introductory Essay: The Fourth Voice of Poetry" (by John
Hall Wheelock, the prefatory piece to *Good News of Death and
Other Poems*), Simpson is quoted as having said this of his work:

"These poems are parts of my life. I have, like most men, made journeys,
and have loved; like most men of my generation, I have seen or heard of
wars. I do not apologize in these poems for my own experience, nor do I
feel these things have been said before. Indeed, as they happened to me,
they have never before been said by anyone. That is why I have written
the poems. I have kept the lines clean of words and references that have
to be looked up. Each poem explains itself. No Chinese, no footnotes. In
'Good News of Death' [the twelve-page title piece] I have even taken
care to tell who Orestes was, at the risk of telling the scholar what he
already knows. The poems were not written for scholars, but for common people. I once thought of calling them Lyric and Dramatic Poems.
They are lyric in manner: the sound is the form—the sound gives a
dimension of feeling. Dramatic: because the poems deal, more or less,
with a Dramatic or human situation, as opposed to metaphysics, literature or a transitory mood."

Everywhere apparent in *Good News of Death and Other
Poems,* Simpson's expertise as a craftsman is not simply his ability
to handle meter and rhyme effectively; in addition, both images
and rhythms contribute to intensity and meaning more so than in
the majority of poems in *The Arrivistes.* Mona Van Duyn, in the
August, 1956, number of *Poetry,* summarizes well the qualities
reviewers of the volume single out for mention: "These are suave
and polished poems, very fine ones. One would have to search
hard to find any stumbling in metrics or imagery. To describe
them, one thinks of such terms as intellectual, witty, under-
stated." In a few of the poems Simpson works toward the natural
qualities of a colloquial language that, with the 1963 publication
of *At the End of the Open Road,* signals Simpson's departure from
the formal in poetry.

Certain poems should be noted for their technical accomplishments. Perhaps "The True Weather for Women," a satire on young, middle-class American women of the 1950s who are only concerned with the satisfaction of their impulses, is one of the best examples in the volume of a poem that could not have been more effectively expressed if it were written in any other manner than by the strictest adherence to formal elements. In four stanzas of seven iambic pentameter lines, the poem follows a complex, interwoven rhyme pattern that by its subtlety and unobtrusiveness contributes to the poem's rhythmic force. "Memories of a Lost War," like the other war poems of this volume, successfully blends the natural voice of man into a preestablished pattern; in this case, the metrics alternate between iambic pentameter and dimeter, and the rhyme is a standard *a b a b*. The alternating metrics contributes to the same kind of sing-song rhythms that Simpson employs so well in "Arm in Arm" and "Carentan O Carentan" from *The Arrivistes*. In the 125-line "Islanders," which is composed of four parts, Simpson demonstrates his ability to write at ease in both heroic and irregular line-length couplets. "Sleeping Beauty" consists of three eight-line stanzas in which only two syllables are accented per line; the insistent force of the rhythms is augmented by approximate and irregular rhyming. And "The Battle" deserves notice for, among other things, its images. Take, for instance, the following: "Somewhere up ahead / Guns thudded. Like the circle of a throat / The night on every side was turning red."

Two contiguous poems—"American Preludes" and "West"—prefigure stylistically the direction Simpson is to take in his poems of the Emotive Imagination. "American Preludes," the lesser success, begins part 3 with this pre–Emotive Imagination stanza:

> The white walls
> Undulate with sea shadows. In the fields
> The cypresses stand up like somber flames,
> And yellow roses tangle from the walls.

Following a narrative first section, the remaining sections amount to an obscure, surrealistic interpretation of early American history. (In the poems from about 1959 in which Simpson adopts certain surrealistic practices, he is careful not to use referents so personal that the poem is merely imagistic associations privately owned by the poet; in the later poems, he considers the reader's shared experiences.) "West," on the other hand, is a good venture in the colloquial and in having images carry the weight of the poem. America's need for constant movement is juxtaposed with the country's great and ancient redwood trees. The poem closes with lines that, except for the rhyming, could have come from *At the End of the Open Road:*

> On their red columns drowse
> The eagles battered at the Western gate;
> These trees have held the eagles in their state
> When Rome was still a rumor in the boughs.

There is evidence in *A Dream of Governors,* issued in 1959 by Wesleyan University Press, that Simpson is on the edge of breaking from poems built upon meter, rhyme, and regular stanzas. Reviewers, by and large, were pleased with Simpson's new book. Writing in *Encounter* in September, 1960, Donald Hall, who himself has written poems in the tradition of the Emotive Imagination and who has shown a steady interest in Simpson's poetry, has this to say of the volume: "Louis Simpson . . . has written one of the most remarkable of recent American books. I don't believe anyone in recent times has achieved such a synthesis of wild imagination and formal decorum." And the enthusiasm of Anthony Hecht is apparent in this excerpt from his review in the Winter, 1959/60, issue of the *Hudson Review:*

It is hard to realize how consistently excellent and various his work can be without reading carefully through his book again and again. This is one of the best new books of poetry in years. He commands a style capable of great emotional range, at once witty and dramatic, sometimes spare and ironic, sometimes frighteningly phantasmagoric, always inventive and not infrequently beautiful.

There were, of course, critics who were aware that Simpson's wit, sophistication, and use of formal elements served to preclude insight and revelation. Some reviewers of his first two volumes felt the same way; they sensed that Simpson was glittering the surface too brightly and they felt he was severely limiting himself by his commitment to rhyme and meter. In a 1958 article, Bly exhorts Simpson to search for a form as fresh as his content.[3] "Crunk" reiterates his charge in a 1960 essay, citing particularly "The Runner": "The poet is describing new experiences and inner sensations, for which there is no extensive precedent in English poetry, with a rhyme and diction developed in another century for totally different moods and events."[4]

Most of the poems, then, in *A Dream of Governors* verify Simpson's stylistic commitments made in the 1940s: the neat stanza divisions, lines of regular meter, and the ubiquitous rhymes. Naturally, writing within the traditional forms is not by itself either valuable or valueless, and in *A Dream of Governors* Simpson does achieve more success with some poems than with others. "The Green Shepherd," the first poem in the book, consists of thirteen quatrains of rhymed iambic pentameter on the *carpe diem* theme and involving the indifference of two bucolic lovers to events that shaped the destiny of the world. While not a bad poem, it seems to expend much energy on the trivial, and Simpson usually has little truck with the insignificant. On the other hand, "Orpheus in the Underworld," which follows the same rhyme and meter patterns, is a singularly fine poem examining the loss of love. "The Flight to Cytherea," metered, rhymed, and divided into regular stanzas, is a brilliant poem structured by a series of metaphors and involving the speaker's descent into

---

3. Crunk, "The Work of Louis Simpson," *Fifties*, I (1958), 25.
4. Crunk, "Louis Simpson's New Book," *Sixties*, IV (Fall, 1960), 59. Simpson devotes several pages of *North of Jamaica* to a discussion of Robert Bly, in which he mentions that "My tastes in poetry were frequently different from Bly" and yet "my writing was sharpened by our talks." *North of Jamaica* (New York: Harper & Row, 1972), 210–11.

madness and his return to sanity brought about by the regenerative powers of love. In this poem the imagination is loosed; and despite the formal elements, the language is colloquial, as in expressions like "Once, when I felt like that" and "I'm not talking of."

By its exciting metaphoric associations, "The Flight to Cytherea" suggests that Simpson's imagination may be growing too powerful for the confines of externally imposed forms. Its natural speech patterns find parallels in several other poems in the volume, notably "Hot Night on Water Street," "The Boarder," and "The Bird." However, in two poems—"I Dreamed that in a City Dark as Paris" and "Orpheus in America"—there are clear indications of Simpson's experimentation with new diction, rhythms, and methods of perceiving.

Several critics cite the hallucinatory qualities of the poems in *A Dream of Governors*.[5] Certainly, "I Dreamed that in a City Dark as Paris" must have been foremost in the critics' minds when they chose the word *hallucinatory*. And though the poem is committed to iambic pentameter lines and is rhymed irregularly, the internal situation is dramatically different from most of Simpson's poems to date in that the speaker, a soldier in World War II, is dreaming that he "wandered" through the brain of a World War I French soldier. The metaphoric suggestions in the last three lines of the poem—"The violence of waking life disrupts / The order of our death. Strange dreams occur, / For dreams are licensed as they never were"—anticipate the imaginative leaps characterizing Simpson's new departures in poems from *At the End of the Open Road* to the present. The same can be said of the highly metaphoric "The Flight to Cytherea," in which hallucination is also at work, but it is not as readily identifiable as it is in "I Dreamed that in a City Dark as Paris." For the casual reader, "The Flight to Cytherea" is merely "obscure."

5. See Thom Gunn, "Excellence and Variety," *Yale Review*, XLIX (Winter, 1960), 298–99; Crunk, "Louis Simpson's New Book," 58–59; and C. B. Cox, "The Poetry of Louis Simpson," *Critical Quarterly*, VIII (Spring, 1966), 72.

"Orpheus in America" and "Côte d'Azur" are experimental in their near abandonment of all external forms in favor of free verse. The former begins exuberantly—"Here are your meadows, Love, as wide as heaven / Green spirits, leaves / And winds, your ministers"—as Orpheus addresses Eurydice after they have risen safely from the underworld and arrived as early settlers in America. Orpheus' emotional response to the expansiveness and freedom of America is such that it could not be contained in deliberate measures and formal stanzas, though the poem contains some irregular rhyming. "Côte d'Azur" is not metaphoric or imaginatively innovative in its internal structuring, but it is Simpson's most prosy poem in the collection and the one in which he follows most closely the diction and rhythms of natural speech. The opening lines establish the diction and rhythms for the remainder of the poem:

> Christian says, "You know it's Paradise,"
> Mending his net.
> "The English," he says, "for example . . .
> They come and lie in the sun until they are
> As red as that roof.
> And then it's finished. They never recover."

With the 1963 publication of *At the End of the Open Road* by Wesleyan University Press, Simpson's poetry radically changes. The year before, Simpson wrote the following in an anthology entitled *Poet's Choice* as the prose accompaniment to his poem "Walt Whitman at Bear Mountain":

I had recently published a book of poems, *A Dream of Governors,* in which I had solved to my satisfaction certain difficulties of writing "in-form"—that is, in regular meter and rhyme. But now I felt that my skill was a strait-jacket. Also, inevitably, the adoption of traditional forms led me into a certain way of ending a poem, polishing it off, so to speak, that sometimes distorted my real meaning. It was time, I felt, to write a new kind of poem. I wanted to write a poem that would be less "willed." I would let images speak for themselves. The poem would be a statement, of course—there really is no such thing as a poem of pure metaphor or image—but I wanted the statement to be determined by the poem itself, to let my original feeling develop, without confining it in any strict fashion. [6]

Reviewers and critics were quick to notice the change. Writing in 1964, Duane Locke sensibly analyzes Simpson's new method, that of the Emotive Imagination: "In *Open Road,* the style loosens, the lines become uneven, and the movement of the natural voice and phrasal breaks replace preconceived measurement. The imagery tends toward inwardness, and the result is a more phenomenal poetry, one in which the subjective imagination transforms by its own operations the objective into what constitutes genuine reality." [7] (As a minor qualification, it should be pointed out that since 1963 Simpson has published in books three poems in which he uses regular meter and rhyme: "The Riders Held Back" and "My Father in the Night Commanding No" from *At the End of the Open Road* and "Columbus" from the New Poems division of *Selected Poems.)*

In the following discussion concerning Simpson's use of the Emotive Imagination, the representative poems cited come from *At the End of the Open Road,* the New Poems included in *Selected Poems,* and *Adventures of the Letter I.* The techniques Simpson has used since his "conversion" remain constant, with the exception that in the poems from the last volume he has become more conversational, which is in keeping with the more openly biographical nature of that volume. In addition, there will be instances acknowledged of Simpson's use of the Emotive Imagination later in the chapter in the discussion of his major thematic considerations as these are manifest in his poems since 1963.

In its use of personification, juxtaposed images, metaphoric leaps, and in its surprise conclusion, "Outward" is exemplary of the Emotive Imagination:

6. Paul Engle and Joseph Langland (eds.), *Poet's Choice* (New York: Dial Press, Inc., 1962), 218.
7. Duane Locke, "New Directions in Poetry," *dust,* I (Fall, 1964), 68–69.

> The staff slips from the hand
> Hissing and swims on the polished floor.
> It glides away to the desert.
>
> It floats like a bird or lily
> On the waves, to the ones who are arriving.
> And if no god arrives,
>
> Then everything yearns outward.
> The honeycomb cell brims over
> And the atom is broken in light.
>
> Machines have made their god. They walk or fly.
> The towers bend like Magi, mountains weep,
> Needles go mad, and metal sheds a tear.
>
> *
>
> The astronaut is lifted
> Away from the world, and drifts.
> How easy it is to be there!
>
> How easy to be anyone, anything but oneself!
> The metal of the plane is breathing;
> Sinuously it swims through the stars.

The confusion resulting from the apparent irrationality of images is clarified in the section of the poem following the asterisk, in which we learn that an astronaut is in outer space, the fact of which leads the speaker to conclude that self-knowledge is more difficult to gain than knowledge of any other kind.

The imaginative and imagistic structuring of "Outward" is quite removed from the basic method Simpson employs in the greater majority of poems prior to his commitment to the Emotive Imagination. Even the conversational rhythms of the poem generate a tension by the shocking images they carry, images that jolt and confound the reader. Even if not understood rationally by the reader that it is an indictment of America's need to expand, "Outward" still communicates by its emotive power.

"Adam Yankev," "Love, My Machine," "Frogs," and "The Morning Light" are all structured by the juxtaposing of images that culminate in a muted shock or personal revelation at the conclusion. "Adam Yankev" is divided into four sections, the emotive leap occurring in section 4. The speaker, Simpson himself, is drawing upon the fecundity of memory to conjure up an image of his "mother's family [in Russia] sitting around the kitchen stove / arguing—the famous Russian theater." In section 2 he recalls his late teenage years in New York City where "Old men with beards and *yarmelkehs*" and "old women sitting on the benches" reminisced about "their lives in the Old Country." He abruptly juxtaposes this image of serenity with auto headlights hurling "their shadows against the wall," after which in section 3 the speaker recognizes that, as much as he would like to identify with the individuals in his poem, he cannot completely. But at the same time, he exlaims: "I feel I am part of a race / that has not yet arrived in America. / Yet, these people—their faces are strangely familiar." The concluding section of the poem is a gentle lament, with images drawn from the natural world, and provides the muted shock through the essential sameness yet enormous distances between the two cultures:

> The first clear star comes gliding
> over the trees and dark rooftops,
> the same world passing here—
>
> voices and shadows of desire,
> and the tears of things. . . . Around us
> things want to be understood.
>
> And the moon, so softly gleaming
> in furs,
> that put a hole through Pushkin.

At the end of "Love, My Machine," the speaker internalizes a series of images about the immortality of light waves, communication by radio waves, space as an entity, solitude, Gandhi, "Jesus, / Moses, and all the other practical people" by declaring: "By the light of the stars / This night is serious. / I am going into the night to find a world of my own." And in the closing stanza of the fifteen-line poem "Frogs" the speaker announces dramatically: "In the city I pine for the country; / In the country I long for conversation— / Our happy croaking." This poem, which may be a veiled account of poetry itself, brings the speaker in at the end in an imaginative leap, after the twelve preceding lines describing frogs, fireflies, and flowers. "The Morning Light" fuses images from the natural world with the speaker's inward drama; this fusion is enacted movingly in the final stanza:

> Day lifts the darkness from the hills,
> A bright blade cuts the reeds,
> And my life, pitilessly demanding,
> Rises forever in the morning light.

In fact, it is primarily in the conclusions to his poems that Louis Simpson finds the most fertile grounds for the Emotive Imagination method. Poems like "The Climate of Paradise" and "On the Prairie" (the third part of the trilogy "Indian Country") progress by observation through images to a muted shock ending in which significance is revealed. Of course, these are by no means the only poems exemplifying this process.

Even though excerpts from his work cited so far in this chapter suggest the contrary, Simpson's commitment to the rural is in no way comparable to that of Robert Bly, James Wright, or William Stafford. But in a 1964 interview, Simpson does say: "I think a lot of poetry in the last twenty years has been city poetry, but a lot of it is moving out away in people like myself."[8] At least one poem, "A Farm in Minnesota," from the later Emotive Imagination poems, does testify to Simpson's above remark. It begins with a personification that could have been written by Bly, Wright, or Stafford—"The corn rows walk the earth, / crowding like mankind between the fences, / feeding on sun and rain"— then proceeds to a metaphor characteristic of his colleagues in this movement:

---

8. "An Interview with Louis Simpson, Part II," *dust,* I (Winter, 1965), 19.

> And we who tend them
> from the ground up—lieutenants
> of this foot cavalry, leaning on fences
> to watch our green men never move an inch—
> who cares for us?

At any rate, this poem is something of an isolated example.

Simpson does, however, share with Bly, Wright, and Stafford similarities in technique, particularly their beliefs in the efficacy of the image that rises dream-like from the unconscious. Statements by Simpson on images and surrealism are quoted in Part I of this study. But it seems appropriate to conclude this section by calling attention to remarks Simpson made in 1971 with which all the poets of the Emotive Imagination would concur, at least to some extent:

Total poetry, like the total human being, must include so-called rational as well as irrational states—the poem must be logical as well as unpredictable. Images that move us do so because they are connected to logical thought processes which we all share. They are connected to the psyche of the author and an understandable feeling, or idea if you prefer, underlying the poem. Poetry in which there are no dream states is trivial, but dream images may be trivial, also, when they are produced by automatic writing, without a necessary direction by the psyche of the poet. The answer, therefore, seems to be that the poet dreams and produces the images of his dream, but that only by meditation and selection can he discover poetic images—those which move other people. [9]

---

9. "Louis Simpson," *Review,* XXV (Spring, 1971), 37. "Keeping Abreast, Or Homage to Pablo Neruda Perhaps" is a poem Simpson published in *Sixties,* No. 6, but he chose not to include it in any of his volumes of poetry. It is, however, reprinted in *North of Jamaica.* The poem concerns the speaker's meeting with Thomas, "a nice boy from Amherst," who was exhorting the speaker, Simpson himself, to change his ways in both life and poetry. Simpson's ironic attitude toward the boy and his "newness"—newness for its own sake—is unmistakable:

> What did I ever do to Pablo Neruda?
> I cannot take to hanging out in cafés,
> and my Spanish is bad.
> I am incurably addicted to the old kinds of poems.

Simpson's strong commitment to the kind of poetry articulated above may very well account for the relatively few failures in his work in the 1960s and early 1970s. Indeed, of the Emotive Imagination poets, Simpson achieves the highest percentage of success on a poem-by-poem basis.

Louis Simpson's six-line "American Poetry," first published in *At the End of the Open Road,* has been reprinted frequently in essays on current American poetry and in anthologies. It is a curious poem structured entirely by metaphor:

> Whatever it is, it must have
> A stomach that can digest
> Rubber, coal, uranium, moons, poems.
>
> Like the shark, it contains a shoe.
> It must swim for miles through the desert
> Uttering cries that are almost human.

In essence, the first stanza concerns the motley subjects with which modern American poetry must try to come to terms; the second refers to the problem of acceptance poetry faces in America. As R. R. Cuscaden remarks of the first stanza, "Today poetry must be able to digest the indigestible: 'rubber' (jammed freeways, discarded tires in empty lots), 'coal' (world dominated by business, industrial waste), 'moons' (space explorations which break down old myths and open new worlds), and 'poems' (an ironic commentary on the reams and reams of bad poetry being written today)." [10] Add to this "uranium," by which Simpson could be alluding to war, and two additional meanings of "moon" (love and madness), and this stanza cites several of the subjects that have concerned Simpson in the thirty-plus years that he has been writing poetry.

Despite the heterogeneity in subject matter Simpson has undertaken in his poetry, several areas of inquiry have been, more or less, constant ones. In *The Arrivistes, Good News of Death*

---

10. R. R. Cuscaden, "In the Shark's Belly," *Today,* XXI (January, 1966), 14.

and Other Poems, and *A Dream of Governors,* he has produced one
of the most compelling bodies of war poetry written by an American. From 1959 to the 1971 publication of *Adventures of the Letter
I,* war poems are absent from Simpson's work, but in the 1971
volume he turns once again to the subject, prompted undoubtedly
by the war in Southeast Asia. However, the poems on war in this
book are involved with different issues from those that command
his attention in the first three collections. In the volumes through
At the End of the Open Road, love (or the relationship of a man and
woman) is another constant source for poems. After the 1949
publication of *The Arrivistes,* the subject of America—its origins,
character, spirit, ethos, people, and geography—has been
explored by Simpson so thoroughly and with such excellence (in
the poems since 1963) that he may very well be the American poet
of his generation who has come to terms most meaningfully in
defining the country. More recently, Simpson has, like both
Wright and Stafford, focused on the American Indian as a subject
for his America poems. But Simpson expands beyond the definitive boundaries of America; two poems from *At the End of the Open
Road* and an entire section from *Adventures of the Letter I* are
devoted to characters from the Volhynia Province, the area in
Russia from which his mother's relatives came. And, finally, the
poems in *Adventures of the Letter I*, as the title suggests, demonstrate a new inwardness on Simpson's part; lately he has been
writing poems about his childhood in Jamaica and about his six-
month confinement in a mental institution, following World War
II, for delayed combat fatigue.

During World War II, which provided the poet with considerable subject matter, Simpson, serving with the 101st Airborne
Division, was involved in some of the bitterest fighting of the
European theater. For his part in the war, Simpson received the
Bronze Star with an oak leaf cluster and two Purple Hearts. The
early chapters of his only published novel, *Riverside Drive,* in
which the main character, Duncan Bell, resembles Simpson in

many ways, provide a vivid account of Simpson's war experiences, as do passages in *North of Jamaica;* it is interesting to note
the numerous parallels existing between incidents recorded in
the novel and his poems on war. Simpson has also published two
essays on his years in the military. [11]

In the war poems of the first three volumes, certain thematic
considerations recur, one of which concerns Simpson's conception of the infantryman as a child on a school playground super-
vised by adults, a child whose very action on the playground is the
result of an adult's directive. "Arm in Arm," "Carentan O Carentan," and "Memories of a Lost War" all refer to the soldiers
walking in file as if being led onto the playground at recess time.
"Arm in Arm" and "Carentan O Carentan" both comment specifically on the bewilderment of the soldiers at their first encounter with the enemy, at their initiation to death. After the
ambush in the latter poem, the speaker states confusingly:

> I never strolled, nor ever shall
> Down such a leafy lane.
> I never drank in a canal,
> Nor ever shall again.

Once the green soldiers are confronted with the actuality of combat, they are, at least momentarily, unable to distinguish the real
from the unreal. The speaker of "Carentan O Carentan" shifts
tenses repeatedly as he recounts the ambush and his confused
response. And in "Arm in Arm" the confusion between what is
terribly real and what is make-believe is underscored by both the
soldiers' inability to distinguish their own corpses from those
already entombed and by one particular soldier's taking a skull to
task for spying. In both poems, dead or dying officers and NCOs
serve as symbols of authority no longer able to direct the lives of

---

11. See "The Way It Was In the Bulge," *New York Times Magazine* (December 6,
1964), 27–29, 114, 116, 119, 122–24; and "The Making of a Soldier USA," *Harper's
Magazine*, CCXXXII (February, 1966), 76–80.

the soldier-children, thus adding immeasurably to the confusion of the latter. In these poems, as well as in "The Bird," a poem about a German impressed into service in a concentration camp, the soldiers—American and German—are depicted as pawns in a game over which they have no control, the game of war being itself as absurd as the states the soldiers are in.

Even though the soldiers are reduced by war to pathetic children, they still demonstrate an intense desire to live, as exemplified in the following excerpts gleaned respectively from "Memories of a Lost War" and "The Battle":

> The riflemen will wake and hold their breath.
> Though they may bleed
> They will be proud a while of something death
> Still seems to need.

> Most clearly of that battle I remember
> The tiredness in eyes, how hands looked thin
> Around a cigarette, and the bright ember
> Would pulse with all the life there was within.

Several of Simpson's war poems are set after the war; both "Roll" and "Resistance" question the values war forces men to adopt, and in "Roll" the speaker simply has found it impossible to justify why the soldiers died on the Normandy beachhead. "Roll" is, to state it directly, a protest poem, while "Resistance" is concerned with the values in and the purpose of war, as well as with the postwar attitudes people hold toward the war heroes.

In fact, what happens after war is over and the soldiers are expected to return to the normal lives they led prior to combat is another major concern of Simpson. For the most part, Simpson feels, the soldiers are either forgotten, permanently scarred, or alienated from the society they were supposed to be defending. The first three stanzas of "The Heroes" are deceptively flip and ironic; the returning heroes in this dream-vision poem are seen as they disembarked from the ship, gallantly greeted by girls with doughnuts, by women who wanted to "touch their brave wounds and their hair streaked with gray," and by a chaplain who "advised them to watch and to pray." Then the "rapscallions, these sea-sick battalions" were either forgotten or institutionalized from the wounds that marked them both physically and psychologically. The closing stanza reverses the tone dramatically as the speaker, by means of metaphor and innuendo, expresses his disgust at the aftermath of war as it affects soldiers:

> A fine dust has settled on all that scrap metal.
> The heroes were packaged and sent home in parts
> To pluck at a poppy and sew on a petal
> And count the long night by the stroke of their hearts.

"Old Soldier" replaces the ironic wit of "The Heroes" with colloquially insistent rhythms and with images precipitated by a dream the veteran had one night in his room at the institution. The poem ends with ironic understatement after relating what the veteran must have felt once he woke from the "dream of battle":

> He lies remembering: "That's how it was . . ."
> And smiles, and drifts into a youthful sleep
> Without a care. His life is all he has,
> And that is given to the guards to keep.

"Against the Age" is Simpson's bitterest war poem. In the other war poems in his first three volumes, he has avoided the blatantly emotional by employing varying degrees of irony, by carefully selecting images, by depicting soldiers as children, and by creating in several poems a ballad texture. These, however, are abandoned in favor of accusation and argument in which the physical and especially the mental anguish of war's aftermath is emphasized, as the third stanza amply illustrates:

> Our minds are mutilated—*gueules cassées,*
> They walk the night with hood and mask and stick,
> The government won't let them out by day,
> Their ugliness threatens the Republic.

> Our minds are like those violated souls
> That pass in faceless, threatening patrols.

To Simpson there are no heroes in war, nor is there any glamor or glory. In "The Ash and the Oak," a jaunty piece in which the reader is taken on a brief historical tour of the infantry from "When men discovered freedom first / The fighting was on foot" to Verdun and Bastogne, Simpson suggests that war has never been a legitimate entity. However, there were at least some mitigating qualities in war as it was early practiced by the foot soldier. For example, "At Malplaquet and Waterloo / They were polite and proud," and "At Appomattox too, it seems / Some things were understood." Now that the twentieth century is able to provide more effective means of killing than arrows and guns primed "with billets-doux," the complexion of war has changed, and a hero is no more than a fool. Even if Simpson believes there are no heroes, he nevertheless acknowledges that there are individual acts of bravery, citing in "Resistance" Jean Gardère of the French Resistance, who was "cowardly slain" and whose memory now is considerably dimmed.

Thirty-one pages of *A Dream of Governors* are given over to "The Runner," a blank verse narrative about a soldier named Dodd who acts as a messenger during the 101st Airborne's defense of Bastogne. While it is not important in this study to provide a plot summary, the poem is indeed important in any discussion of Simpson and the subject of war, since it summarizes many of the attitudes expressed in the shorter war poems. For example, Dodd becomes a hero purely by accident. When he is wounded his first thought is relief at the prospect of getting out of the war: "I'm wounded! he thought, with a rush of joy." Just as his heroism is accidental, so too is his alleged cowardice, the result of momentary panic that, under the same circumstances, could have seized any member of the platoon. At any rate, the effect of war on the individual is, as Simpson iterates in his other war poems, one of dehumanization in "The Runner" as well. And if not totally dehumanized, the soldiers are reduced to the status of children, as the case is in "Arm in Arm," "Carentan O Carentan," and "The Bird." If in "The Runner" the soldiers do not *act* like children, they are at least treated as if they were. The men are told what to do and when, but rarely are they told why by the officers. And, of course, Simpson's conviction that glory and honor in war are concepts of questionable validity is underscored in the poem by the nature of Dodd's accidental heroism.

Clearly, Simpson's war poems discussed so far and included in *The Arrivistes, Good News of Death and Other Poems,* and *A Dream of Governors* for the most part focus on the situation of the individual soldier. Since the 1959 publication of *A Dream of Governors,* Simpson has written World War II and the individual soldier out of his poetry. There is one poem, "American Dreams," first published in the Spring, 1960, issue of *Listen,* that deals with war on a rather abstract level. Simpson included it in *Adventures of the Letter I* in 1971, having apparently decided that it was not right for either *At the End of the Open Road* or *Selected Poems.* Since 1966, "American Dreams," which is reproduced below, has been reprinted a number of times, probably because it could be read as a protest to the American presence in Southeast Asia:

> In dreams my life came toward me,
> my loves that were slender as gazelles.
> But America also dreams. . . .
> Dream, you are flying over Russia,
> dream, you are falling in Asia.
>
> As I look down the street
> on a typical sunny day in California
> it is my house that is burning
> and my dear ones that lie in the gutter
> as the American army enters.
>
> Every day I wake far away
> from my life, in a foreign country.
> These people are speaking a strange language.

> It is strange to me
> and strange, I think, even to themselves.

One is probably right in assuming that the U-2 incidents of the 1950s occasioned the poem, though its prophetic implications cannot be denied.

The haunting context of "American Dreams" is similar to the atmosphere of two brief portions of poems in *Adventures of the Letter I* dealing with American involvement in Vietnam: "On the Eve" ends ominously: "and ships, wrapped in a mist, / creep out with their heavy secrets / to the war 'that no one wants'." "A Friend of the Family" carries this indictment:

> And those who are still distending the empire
> have vanished beyond our sight.
> Far from the sense of hearing
> and touch, they are merging
> with Asia . . .
>
> expanding the war on nature
> and the old know-how to Asia.

Finally, in "Doubting" the speaker sadly laments:

> And there's no end, it seems, to the wars of democracy.
> What would Washington, what would Jefferson say
> of the troops so heavily armed?
>
> They would think they were Hessians,
> and ride back into the hills
> to find the people that they knew.

The few instances cited above, including "American Dreams," can in no way classify Simpson as a poet now actively involved in the subject of war. On the other hand, the poems from his first three volumes do indeed place him among the most effective interpreters of the war experience.

Although Simpson will never be classed as a major love poet, he has written rather extensively, especially in the poems through *At the End of the Open Road,* on the subject of love and on the relationship between a man and woman. By having been reprinted in subsequent volumes, three love lyrics from *The Arrivistes* have survived: "Summer Storm," "The Custom of the World" (originally titled "A Witty War" and then revised), and "Song: 'Rough Winds Do Shake the Darling Buds of May.' "

The most compelling feature of Simpson's earlier love lyrics is the enigmatic, elusive character of the woman, who is in fact a poetized version of Mona Jocelyn, the sensual girl/woman in Simpson's novel, *Riverside Drive*. In large part, the novel is the story of a consuming love affair between Duncan Bell, the narrator and mask for Simpson, and Mona. The two excerpts reproduced below provide the reader with a capsule portrait of the many-faceted Mona. The first describes her at fourteen, the second after Duncan and Mona have parted permanently:

Mona had the word "illicit" written on her brow. She was the kind for whom as she approached old ladies opened their bags, got out their wool, and started knitting the letter A. Young men when she passed by fell silent, staring at her. Old men from Vienna, sitting on park benches, remembering cups of chocolate with whipped cream, a glass of brandy, a cigar—those old men when Mona went by dreamed dreams; they visited their little opera dancer again, and piece by piece, removed her lace and slippers; and the music on the phonograph was Offenbach's.

*   *   *   *

When I think of Mona, I see a number of women who, by some chance, have the features of one woman, as though the artist had only one idea of a nose, of eyes and ears, through which to show a variety of lives. As for cause and effect, chronology, it doesn't exist; or rather, it depends on the way I move the light. One of these women is chaste; another is unfaithful; a third is intelligent; a fourth is stupid. . . . When I think of Mona, pleasure and boredom, trust and suspicion, love and hatred, exist side by side, rapidly succeeding or merging into one another. Sometimes the light moves back again to fasten on a detail. And then, areas of the painting have faded.

The following poems, in one way or another, concern a woman who possesses characteristics similar to Mona's or involve the relation of a man (like Duncan Bell) and Mona: "Summer Storm" and "Song: 'Rough Winds Do Shake the Darling Buds of May'" from *The Arrivistes;* "A Woman Too Well Remembered," "The Man Who Married Magdalene," and "Sleeping Beauty" from *Good News of Death and Other Poems;* "The Lover's Ghost" and "The Custom of the World" from *A Dream of Governors* (one section is entitled Love Poems); and perhaps "Summer Morning" from *At the End of the Open Road.* These poems explore Mona's contradictory nature, celebrate her sensuality and the domain of physical love, sometimes in an ironic manner, and dramatize the speaker's anger toward and desire for Mona. In "A Woman Too Well Remembered," for example, the speaker realizes there is more to the woman than he can possibly know. He asks, "Then is she simply false, and falsely fair?" but, like Duncan Bell, he does not know. Yet he is inexorably attracted to her: "For when the stars move like a steady fire / I think of her, and other faces fade." It is interesting that in both "The Man Who Married Magdalene" and "Sleeping Beauty" the woman in question is imaged as a prostitute.

Even if Mona is the girl in the poem "Summer Morning," she is absent from Simpson's love poems included in *At the End of the Open Road* and in his subsequent writings. This suggests that, at least as far as his poetry is concerned, Simpson has been able to extricate the Mona figure from his mind. Norman Friedman argues that the four love poems that begin part 2 of *At the End of the Open Road*—"Summer Morning," "The Silent Lover," "Birch," and "The Sea and the Forest"—"far transcend in passion, sensuality, and significance his earlier group of love poems."[12]

12. Norman Friedman, "The Wesleyan Poets—II," *Chicago Review,* XIX (1966), 71. By "earlier group" Friedman means those poems included in *A Dream of Governors,* since his essay concerns only those volumes of poetry issued by Wesleyan University Press. However, the Love Poems section of the book does include several lyrics from *The Arrivistes.* Unfortunately, Friedman did not have the Mona poems from *Good News of Death and Other Poems* before him.

The four from *At the End of the Open Road* are in colloquial language, but with Simpson this does not mean that lyrical effects must necessarily be precluded. He has the ability to infuse lines with the rhythmic motion appropriate to both subject and attitude. Certainly, the new love poems differ in direction and in degree of imagination from the earlier ones, and each ends with the metaphoric leap characteristic of the Emotive Imagination, by which Simpson both extends and clarifies meaning. In "Summer Morning" and "The Sea and the Forest," the speakers themselves are the primary objects of the leaps; in "The Silent Lover" and "Birch" the speaker's perceptions are the objects.

"Summer Morning," a poem which the reviewer in the June 18, 1964, *Times Literary Supplement* calls a "closely felt poem about change bringing horror of illusory freedom," ends with the line, "My life that I hold in secret." This is the speaker's lament for his own inability to feel any degree of commitment with a woman now. "The Sea and the Forest" is not, as such, a love poem; rather, it concerns the responses a French woman elicits from sailors on the deck of a ship and from the speaker himself, who, by the end of the poem, exclaims, "Farewell, my own pine forest! / I might have lived there for a thousand years." The speaker has created an imaginative world so pleasing and delightful as a result of the woman's presence that he could remain there forever. "Birch" is a good short lyric structured by metaphor; the appropriateness of the comparison is clarified in the last stanza:

> Birch tree, you remind me
> Of a room filled with breathing,
> The sway and whisper of love.
>
> She slips off her shoes;
> Unzips her skirt; arms raised,
> Unclasps an earring, and the other.
>
> Just so the sallow trunk
> Divides, and the branches
> Are pale and smooth.

The conclusion of "The Silent Lover" is a gentle fusion of all elements of the seashore where the poem is set:

> I think the rustling of her clothes
> Is like the sea, and she
> A wild white bird.
>
> And love is like the sighing of the sand.

There are several poems from *Adventures of the Letter I* in which love is mentioned or in which the relationship of a man and woman is considered. "Love and Poetry," for instance, begins with "My girl the voluptuous creature," proceeds to draw analogies between poetry and virtually everything else, and concludes in this hardly romantic manner: "The bitches! They want to feel wanted, / and everything else is prose." But only one lyric, "Sensibility," belongs genuinely in the category of a love poem:

> Her face turned sour.
> It broke into tears.
> She wept, she wept.
> The streams were wide and deep.
> Wide and deep were the streams
> of time that were flowing toward me.
> Neither she nor I could control
> the flow of her tears,
> and so, in the middle of summer,
> this tender girl and I
> were married in rain-water.

Louis Simpson was born in Jamaica, where he spent his first seventeen years. Since 1940, except for his military service in Europe and for several years spent on grants and awards to study and write in Europe, he has remained in America, which granted him citizenship after he was released from the army. While in Jamaica, he always felt that there was a larger world waiting for him to discover. A quotation from an interview cited in Part I, Chapter 1, by Simpson documents his interest in and enthusiasm about America. As far as Simpson's literary career is concerned, his coming to America is the single most important event of his life. The first stanza of "Port Jefferson" speaks to the issues of his coming to America and of his ability to interpret the country so incisively:

> My whole life coming to this place
> and understanding it better
> maybe for having been born
> offshore, and at an early age
> left to my own support. . . . [13]

And in 1962 Simpson said: "I think a great deal about the country I live in; indeed, it seems an inexhaustible subject, one that has hardly been tapped. By America, I mean the infinitely complex life we have." [14]

Though Simpson admits an intense excitement about America on his arrival in 1940, he does not use the country as a subject for poems in his first volume. It is not until the 1955 publication of *Good News of Death and Other Poems* that the country becomes the source for several poems, and these, by and large, do not probe deeply into the condition of America. His early poems on America are important, however, for they seek to establish some of the basic attitudes that the poet is later to explore in greater depth. One of the problems in his early poems on the subject must necessarily relate to his being bound at the time by the formal elements of poetry; for when he abandons them in the poems after *A Dream of Governors,* he is able to write some of the most impressive poems of his generation on America. And there are other reasons that will be explained shortly in this chapter.

13. Simpson's father died when the boy was in his late teens. Aston Simpson was a wealthy lawyer in Jamaica; however, by some turn never understood by Simpson himself, he was left virtually nothing in the estate. His mother and father were separated when the boy was six or seven, and his father subsequently remarried. Simpson told Ronald Moran in 1969 that the poem "On the Lawn at the Villa" was occasioned by a visit he paid to his mother after he had not seen her for many years. At any rate, when he reached New York City in 1940, Simpson had to fend for himself.

14. Engle and Langland (eds.), *Poet's Choice,* 219.

Four poems from *Good News of Death and Other Poems* concern America: "Mississippi," "Islanders," "American Preludes," and "West." Since in "Mississippi" Simpson is content to rely on stock associations of the river and the Old South, his attempt to define attitudes held in the American past simply does not work. In "Islanders" he uses the mask method similar to the use T. S. Eliot puts it to in "The Love Song of J. Alfred Prufrock"; in addition, the rhythms, the image of hypocrisy in the city, and the study of an alienated man owe debts to Eliot's poem.[15] Even though the poem is itself more about the origin and purpose of poetry, it still approaches the subject of America by questioning the American spirit of restlessness, by describing New York City at night as "sinister for miles" with its mammoth, darkened skyscrapers, by indicating the exploitation of workmen in the city, by using the automobile as a symbol for the American urge for speed, and by the following passage from part 3, in which Simpson's attitude toward America at this point in his career is exemplified:

> The blind man counts the nickels in his cup,
> But eyes go flying sideways, flying up
> Like dazzled birds. Besides the daily wage
> They're caught in their own lives, the inner cage,
> And cry for exits, hoping to be shown
> A way by others, who have lost their own.

Both "American Preludes" and "West" from *Good News of Death and Other Poems* are mentioned earlier in this chapter as precursors to Simpson's later style. Of the two, "West" is the

---

15. "Eliot has certainly been a continuing influence on my work." Louis Simpson in a letter to Ronald Moran, March 9, 1971. Eliot is mentioned a number of times in *North of Jamaica,* but not in an influence context. The autobiography does record the time when Robert Bly and Simpson accompanied Donald Hall in New York when Hall was assigned to interview Eliot. Some of Simpson's comments on Eliot are of interest:

I was conscious that I was looking at the most important literary man of the last forty years. And one of the great poets in English. If the age were to be named after one man, it would probably be Eliot. . . . Eliot . . . had the ability actually to create in images the things he was talking about, and architectonic power, the ability to draw things together. *North of Jamaica,* 238–39.

more important poem. Where "American Preludes" fails in its surrealistic, incoherent sections that follow the narrative opening, "West" is successful in calling attention to America's need for movement, which is evident in the opening lines: "On US 101/I felt the traffic running like a beast,/Roaring in space." This scene of confusion is set in opposition to the serenity of Mount Tamalpais, which overlooks the Pacific Ocean and San Francisco Bay; the mountain with its redwoods is metaphorically called the "red princess" that "slopes / In honeyed burial from hair to feet." The contrast of automobiles with the magnificent redwoods introduces what become in *At the End of the Open Road* two recurrent symbols. And the state of California becomes for Simpson the setting for his most significant poems on America.

The opening poem of the My America section of *A Dream of Governors* is "To the Western World":

> A siren sang, and Europe turned away
> From the high castle and the shepherd's crook.
> Three caravels went sailing to Cathay
> On the strange ocean, and the captains shook
> Their banners out across the Mexique Bay.
>
> And in our early days we did the same.
> Remembering our fathers in their wreck
> We crossed the sea from Palos where they came
> And saw, enormous to the little deck,
> A shore in silence waiting for a name.
>
> The treasures of Cathay were never found.
> In this America, this wilderness
> Where the axe echoes with a lonely sound,
> The generations labor to possess
> And grave by grave we civilize the ground.

There is some fine writing in this poem, notably the last two lines in the second stanza and the last three lines in the final stanza; yet "To the Western World" lacks the vision and depth that distinguish the later America poems.

In one way or another, four of the poems in the My America

section cite television or movies in symbolic contexts as indices of the American mind that needs programed entertainment. "Hot Night on Water Street" focuses sharply on scenes in a small American town somewhere on the Ohio River across from the West Virginia border. The concept of motion pictures leads the speaker to this ironic indictment: "Some day, when this uncertain continent / Is marble, and men ask what was the good / We lived by, dust may whisper 'Hollywood.' " And in "The Boarder," which like "Hot Night on Water Street" is concerned with the theme of man's alienation in an American town, the speaker refers to the "TV sets [that] have been turned on." "The Boarder" ends suggestively and on a lonely note:

> But the pale stranger in the furnished room
>   Lies on his back
> Looking at paper roses, how they bloom,
>   And ceilings crack.

"Landscape with Barns" develops through a series of contrasts the dream America cherishes about itself. In the first stanza, the speaker calls attention to various elements indigenous to the American way of life: industry, the automobile, and the farmhouse where "we watch TV / While moonlight falls in silence, drop by drop." Then as the poem progresses, the dream becomes the major thematic consideration:

> The country that Columbus thought he found
> Is called America. It looks unreal,
> Unreal in winter and unreal in summer.
> When movies spread their giants on the air
> The boys drive to the next town, drunk on nothing.
> Youth has the secret. Only death looks real.

Although the poem "Mediterranean" is included in the Old World section of *A Dream of Governors,* it is about America. Set across the bay from Cannes while the annual film festival is in progress, the poem's speaker can also hear television sets roaring "from the villas on the shore." He is repelled by the Americanization of France symbolized by both the movies and the television sets:

> And since this is the case in France
> I have obtained a rubber boat.
> As these advantages advance
> I'll grow increasingly remote.
> The water laps around the bow.
> Goodbye. For I am leaving now.

Simpson's reliance on surface irony, such as that evidenced above, is one of the reasons the America poems prior to those included in *At the End of the Open Road* are weaker than the later ones in which the techniques of the Emotive Imagination are employed.

One poem in *A Dream of Governors,* "Orpheus in America," is an exception, primarily because it probes by images of imaginative power more deeply into the subject of America. Orpheus pictures America (or the thought of America) as a continent holding great promise for Eurydice, to whom the poem is addressed, and himself. Yet Orpheus is aware, too, that America *may only be* "a desert with a name"; however, its possibilities excite him, and he concludes his address in these metaphorically charged lines:

> Another world is here, a greener Thrace!
> Here are your meadows, Love, as wide as heaven,
> Green spirits, leaves
> And winds, your ministers,
> In this America, this other, happy place.

With the 1963 publication of *At the End of the Open Road* and in his poems since then, Simpson has taken on the subject of America with an intensity and perceptual depth unmatched by any other of the Emotive Imagination poets. In 1959 he moved from New York to California, which was then viewed as an American Garden of Eden, an image that recurs in several of his poems. Simpson found in the state of California—with its emphasis on promises to be fulfilled, materialism, and the physical life of pleasure—an ordering device for his poems. In a 1972 essay incorporated into *North of Jamaica,* Simpson reflects on the years he spent in California:

All the time I lived in California I felt that I was carrying out a Whitmanesque experiment, trying to digest the landscape he had written about—though he had traveled no further west than the Mississippi. In spite of my antipathy for the Californians, their mindless pleasure-seeking and their fear and envy of anything that came from outside, yet I felt that I could find words for the reality of the place. This was only a feeling, and I could not talk to other people about what I felt."[16]

Later in the autobiography, Simpson is more charged in his response to the state:

O God, O California! There was probably no place in the world that had better scenery, and there was no sadder place in the world either. Here were all the disconnected people—farmers from Iowa who had lived in mud and now wanted only to doze in the sunshine; young women from Brooklyn with warts, whose politics were purely revenge; the children of swimming-pools in La Jolla and tennis courts in Connecticut. At night across the Bay the lights of Fairyland twinkled and beckoned. Here came all the lost people, to the end of America where there is nowhere to go but out of your mind.[17]

In addition, Simpson's move to California seemed to coincide with his rediscovery in the poetry of Walt Whitman an attempt to embrace and define America as well as the stylistic abandonment in Whitman's very act of embracing and defining. It is perhaps possible to place too much emphasis on Whitman's influence on Simpson's own qualified stylistic abandon, for Simpson's own poetry evidences a much more careful craftsman at work. The influence, rather the force, of Whitman on Simpson lies primarily in subject choice and attitude, more exactly in providing

16. Louis Simpson, "O California! A Poet's Notes on the Sixties" *The Columbia Forum,* NS I (Summer, 1972), 26. Also included in *North of Jamaica,* 224–25.
17. Simpson, *North of Jamaica,* 269.

Simpson with a way of perceiving America. Of course, Simpson is not the celebrator Whitman is. Simpson has said of the author of *Leaves of Grass:* "Whitman means a great deal to me. When I came to America at the age of seventeen, an intelligent cousin gave me a copy of *Leaves of Grass.* I recognized immediately that Whitman was a great, original poet. I now think he is the greatest poet we have had in America."[18] Writing ten years later, Simpson still finds much in Whitman to admire, but he admits in prose, as he does in his poem "Lines Written Near San Francisco," that he questions seriously Whitman's ideas:

He was the best and worst of poets. . . . "Song of Myself" was the greatest poem yet written by an American. I found Whitman's ideas often intolerable; celebrating progress and industry as ends in themselves was understandable in 1870, for at that time material expansion was also a spiritual experience, but in the twentieth century the message seemed out of date. The mountains had been crossed, the land had been gobbled up, and industry was turning out more goods than people could consume. Also, the democracy Whitman celebrated, the instinctive rightness of the common man, was very much in doubt. Now we were governed by the rich, and the masses were hopelessly committed to an economy based on war. It was a curious thing that a man could write great poetry and still mistaken in his ideas.[19]

At any rate, in several very important poems, both California and Whitman offer Simpson ordering devices. Naturally, the techniques of the Emotive Imagination have permitted Simpson to explore America in colloquial terms and by images that "move with the logic of dreams."

In the four California/Whitman poems from *At the End of the Open Road*—"In California," "Walt Whitman at Bear Mountain," "Pacific Ideas—A Letter to Walt Whitman," and "Lines Written Near San Francisco"—several thematic considerations concerning America are evident. The first is that materialism,

18. Engle and Langland (eds.), *Poet's Choice,* 219.
19. Simpson, "O, California! A Poet's Notes on the Sixties," 26. Also included in *North of Jamaica,* 222.

often symbolized in the figures of bankers and realtors, is responsible for developing America in a manner that can only lead to its eventual downfall. It finds voice in these trenchant lines from "In California":

> Let the realtors divide the mountain,
> For they have already subdivided the valley.
>
> Rectangular city blocks astonished
> Herodotus in Babylon,
> Cortez in Tenochtitlan,
> And here's the same old city-planner, death.

Great empires perish; the "same old city-planner, death" is working on the American empire as it did on the Mesopotamian and Aztec empires. In "Walt Whitman at Bear Mountain," Simpson's finest poem and one of the most significant statements about America in mid–twentieth-century poetry, Simpson indicts those who "contracted / American dreams," for they have erected a country of "grave weight." Once Americans realize this, as Simpson did in an imagined dialogue his speaker carries on with the statue of Whitman at Bear Mountain State Park in New York, then Americans can build the country anew. As Simpson once wrote in a letter concerning "Walt Whitman at Bear Mountain": "Americans might try not being so expansive, for a change; not being programmed for empire."[20] And in "Lines Written Near San Francisco," a poem in part concerned with the efforts to rebuild San Francisco after the earthquake and fire of 1906, the speaker laments the ways in which the reconstruction is being carried out: "Say, did your fathers cross the dry Sierras / To build another London? / Do Americans always have to be second-rate?" But the workmen pay no attention to the speaker. ("The mortar sets—banks are the first to stand.") The following comes from the same poem:

20. Simpson to Ronald Moran, August 3, 1967.

While we were waiting for the land
They'd finished it—with gas drums
On the hilltops, cheap housing in the valleys

Where lives are mean and wretched.
But the banks thrive and the realtors
Rejoice—they have their America.

According to Simpson, one of the great problems in America is the country's need to emulate great societies of the past. In "Walt Whitman at Bear Mountain," the speaker comments that we are so caught up in historical emulation that we are deaf to the real sounds our country wants us to hear:

Then all the realtors,
Pickpockets, salesmen, and the actors performing
Official scenarios,
Turned a deaf ear. . . .

America is heading for the kind of destruction great empires in the past experienced. To this end, as the speaker argues in "Lines Written Near San Francisco," we are not colonists of the English. Rather, "we are the colonists of Death." Our promise is death, "the land / The pioneers looked for"; our pioneers, our forefathers, shaded "their eyes / Against the sun—a murmur of serious life"; and Americans in their technological, materialistic culture are following the steps of their forefathers, who were deceived into believing America was something it was not.

With America's desperate need for motion and its being "programmed for empire," it is frustrated now that it has reached the end of its physical frontier. "Out there on the Pacific / There's no America but the Marines," the speaker of "Lines Written Near San Francisco" ironically comments, while the speaker of "In California" states that "the white row of the Marina / Faces the Rock." What remains fronting San Francisco Bay is Alcatraz, the rock. Since there is nowhere else to go (at the time Simpson wrote

these poems space exploration had not yet been a major effort),
Americans have been turning back inland and have carved the
land into housing subdivisions and the like. In "Walt Whitman at
Bear Mountain" the speaker announces flatly, "The Open Road
goes to the used-car lot," suggesting that the promises once held,
if indeed they were the right promises, have been compromised by
America's settling for the second-rate.

Where, then, does America go? What can it do? Part of the
answer is found in the following from "Lines Written Near San
Francisco": "The land is within. / At the end of the open road we
come to ourselves." First, Americans must recognize that their
only genuine hope for happiness resides in the awareness that the
dreams the country nourished itself upon—success predicated on
the Puritan ethic restated as the Protestant ethic and culminat-
ing in a materialistic empire—were the wrong dreams. Once this
awareness is achieved, as it is by the speaker of "Walt Whitman at
Bear Mountain," then a great relief is felt:

> All that grave weight of America
> Cancelled! Like Greece and Rome.
> The future in ruins!
> The castles, the prisons, the cathedrals
> Unbuilding, and roses
> Blossoming from the stones that are not there. . . .
>
> The clouds are lifting from the high Sierras,
> The Bay mists clearing.
> And the angel in the gate, the flowering plum,
> Dances like Italy, imagining red.

The closing four lines are, in addition to verbalizing this relief,
exemplary of the Emotive Imagination. The images work on the
reader independently of the rational content. He *feels* that something is being illuminated, but he is not exactly certain what.
In the letter from Simpson cited shortly before, the poet explains:

The point of the argument is that Americans might try not being so expansive for a change; not being programmed for empire. If they waited, then, as Rilke suggests in the Duino elegies, "happiness" might fall. A Renaissance is graceful. Then the "angel in the gate"—here symbolized as a plum tree, a color that is given, not created by an act of will—would rejoice. My angel is the dance of "the given" (though . . . it was suggested also by the old angel of Eden, driving man out to a life of will. Here, if you like, the angel's job is over).[21]

Adventures of the Letter I contains two poems in which Whitman's presence is strongly felt. In "Doubting" Simpson contrasts the exuberant feelings he had when he first came to America with those he holds now; and, at one point, Simpson has his speaker assume the identity of Whitman commenting on America as it now is. Since the passage in question is rather lengthy, a brief excerpt will suffice to illustrate Simpson's conception of Whitman's stance: "I am developing backward areas. / I look on the negro as myself, I accuse myself / of sociopathic tendencies, I accuse my accusers." The poem "Sacred Objects" was written to celebrate Whitman's birthday observance at the Huntington Library in 1969; and though one is uncertain about the identity of the "you" to whom the second part of the poem is addressed, the section itself is replete with allusions to Whitman and his poetry. The section is, as well, squarely within the manner of the Emotive Imagination:

> The light that shines through the *Leaves*
> is clear: 'to form individuals.'
>
> A swamp where the seabirds brood.
> When the psyche is still and the soul does nothing,
> a Sound, with shining tidal pools and channels.
>
> And the kingdom is within you . . .
> the hills and all the streams
> running west to the Mississippi.

21. *Ibid.*

There the roads are lined with timothy
and the clouds are tangled with the haystacks.

Your loves are a line of birch trees.
When the wind flattens the grass, it
shines, and a butterfly
writes dark lines on the air.

There are your sacred objects,
the wings and gazing eyes
of the life you really have.

Simpson's major thematic considerations on the subject of America are interwoven in the California/Whitman poems, but they also find voices in other poems since 1963. "On the Lawn at the Villa," though not a California/Whitman poem, opens with an allusion to Whitman, then reprehends America for its materialistic nature: "It's complicated, being an American, / Having the money and the bad conscience, both at the same time." The American middle class, the suburbanite group, is the subject of "The Inner Part," an ironic poem echoing Simpson's belief that America's need for feeling superior will be a factor responsible for its eventual destruction. In "There Is," which like "The Inner Part" is an Emotive Imagination poem, the speaker examines the consummate sadness of his own life and the lives of other Americans. "A Friend of the Family," the longest and one of the most significant poems in *Adventures of the Letter I,* brings together a number of Simpson's familiar themes and attitudes concerning America. In the villas of California, "with swimming-pools shaped like a kidney / technicians are beating their wives. / They're accusing each other of mental cruelty." Meanwhile, in part 2 of this five-part poem, the speaker tells us that materialism has led America into serious trouble: "The dynamo howls / but the psyche is still, like an Indian."

For those not caught up in America's plunge into greatness, wealth, and the acquisition of possessions, Simpson has sympathy. In "Walt Whitman at Bear Mountain," the only ones spared the charge of having contracted the disease of American dreams are "the man who keeps a store on a lonely road, / And the housewife who knows she's dumb, / And the earth." The speaker of "A Friend of the Family" indeed is sincere when he says: "Once upon a time in California / the ignorant married the inane / and they lived happily ever after." The poem "A Farm in Minnesota" contrasts unfavorably the children ("who prefer a modern house") of the farmers, who speak the poem as "we," with the farmers themselves. The moving conclusion to "A Farm in Minnesota" is unusual for Simpson:

> But when our heads are planted
> under the church, from those empty pods
> we rise in the fields of death,
> and are gathered by angels
> and shine in the hands of God.

The title Indian Country, which Simpson names the second division of *Adventures of the Letter I,* refers to America itself, though there are three poems in the division that involve the American Indian: "Indian Country," "Ballad of Another Ophelia," and "The Climate of Paradise." The American Indian is not a subject new to Simpson, for "The Marriage of Pocahontas," an unimpressive poem of eleven pages that Simpson wisely excludes from *Selected Poems,* first appears in *At the End of the Open Road.* And "Black Kettle Raises the Stars and Stripes," part 2 of "Indian Country," is first printed as a separate piece in the New Poems section of *Selected Poems.*

In "The Shadow-hunter" and "On the Prairie," parts 1 and 3 of "Indian Country," Simpson's diction and rhythms are at times remarkably close to those of William Stafford, who has written extensively on the American Indian. The main argument of the triology, "Indian Country," concerns the mistreatment of the Indians at the hands of the white man. "Ballad of Another Ophelia" is a brief poem in the manner of the Emotive Imagination, while "The Climate of Paradise" interestingly contrasts the concepts of Indian gods inhabiting Mt. Shasta with Americans who are "haunted by Red China— / bugles—a sky lit with artillery." In the manner again of the Emotive Imagination, "The Climate of Paradise" proceeds by a series of metaphors involving caves, the concluding one the recesses of the human mind: "O even in Paradise / the mind would make its own winter."

The first section of *Adventures of the Letter I*, Volhynia Province, is prefaced by the following:

When I was a child we lived in a house called Volyn, after Volhynia, the part of Russia where my mother was born. Volhynia was the greatest imaginable distance from the island [Jamaica] on which we lived. It snowed a great deal in Volhynia; there were wolves, Cossacks, and gypsies.

Since then I have learned that the people of Volhynia were poor and afraid of many things. They died in epidemics, the "Volhynia fever" for which the province is noted in medical dictionaries. Yet some of them were scholars and cigarette-smoking intellectuals.

I have come to think of the country around Lutsk, where my mother's people lived, as a muddy plain with a dismal climate. Yet recently I met a Polish drama-critic who remembered spending a fortnight on a river near Lutsk canoeing with a girl. She was dressed like a Viennese and carried a blue parasol.

Thus with this volume Simpson's interest in his real and imagined ancestors in Russia becomes a consuming one, yet there are two earlier poems—"A Story about Chicken Soup" and "The Troika"—from *At the End of the Open Road* in which Simpson's heritage and remembered past play significant roles. The former is involved with the guilt the speaker feels for his own life of relative ease and luxury compared with the lives his ancestors were forced to endure. "The Troika," like "A Story about Chicken Soup," brings in Simpson's own participation in World War II, a participation that brought him to the continent of his ancestors. "The Troika" is a symbolic dream odyssey backwards in time and is exemplary of the Emotive Imagination by its seemingly irrational structure of a series of epiphanies by which the realm of fantasy is entered.

The Volhynia Province poems of *Adventures of the Letter I* combine fantasy, pathos, humor, and the ordinary lives of the people in Odessa into a series of fascinating portraits. Underlying these poems is Simpson's lament for never having been able to know firsthand these individuals: Dvoyna, Avram, Meyer, Isidor, and others. In these pieces, Simpson is always the speaker; and at times he tries through his poetry to breach the gap of time and distance separating them from him, as the opening stanza to "Dvonya" illustrates:

> In the town of Odessa
> there is a garden
> and Dvonya is there,
> Dvonya whom I love
> though I have never been in Odessa.

Dvonya is, we learn as the poem progresses, Simpson's cousin twice removed. His maternal grandfather and grandmother are the subjects of "A Night in Odessa." Meyer, in the poem of that name, was a student who joined the Communist party and was subsequently murdered. Simpson says at the end of the poem:

> Last night I dreamed of Meyer. . . .
>
> He turned his head and smiled.
> With his hand he made a sign . . .
> then his features changed, he was mournful,
> and I heard him say in a clear voice,
> 'Beware! These men killed Meyer.'

In part 4 of "A Friend of the Family," a poem not included in the Volhynia Province section, Simpson addresses the contemporary Russian poet Andrei Voznesensky in these lines which indicate the extent to which Simpson has become involved with the people from Volhynia Province:

> Andrei, all my life I've been haunted
> by Russia—a plain,
> a cold wind from the *shtetl*.
>
> I can hear the wheels of the train.

It is going to Radom,
it is going to Jerusalem. . . .

In the night where candles shine
I have a luminous family . . .
people with their arms round each other

forever.

Commenting in 1962 about "Walt Whitman at Bear Mountain," Simpson states that the poem "springs from an actual experience, as do most of my poems."[22] One remembers as early as 1955 Simpson's having said of his work: "These poems are parts of my life. . . . I do not apologize in these poems for my own experience." Yet the poems prior to those of *Adventures of the Letter I,* despite the subjectivity inherent in the method of the Emotive Imagination, are characterized by a distancing between the poet and his persona. Of course, the title of the most recent collection, presumably a play on Wallace Stevens' "The Comedian as the Letter C," announces formally his turning inward to the personal.

This turning inward, other than in the Volhynia Province poems, is manifested primarily in two other areas of inquiry: Jamaica and his childhood; and his stay in a mental institution. With the exception of "My Father in the Night Commanding No," Simpson had not placed into volumes any poems explicitly concerned with his early years in Jamaica. *Adventures of the Letter I* contains several poems about that country, the best of which is "The Island Mentality," which impugns the superior attitudes held by the colonials toward the natives.

---

22. Engle and Langland (eds.), *Poet's Choice,* 219. In his autobiography, Simpson elaborates on the inception of "Walt Whitman at Bear Mountain":

Meditating my love of Whitman's poems and dislike of his prophecies, I had been thinking of writing a poem about him. Rather, he kept creeping into my poems. While I was still living in the East I had travelled with Robert Bly up the Hudson to Bear Mountain, and there we looked at the statue of Whitman by Jo Davidson. Within a few days I started a poem about it, but I didn't finish the poem until I had been living in California for some time. The fragments then cohered all at once—the way it happens with me if I'm lucky. *North of Jamaica,* 222–23.

Simpson does not remember much of the six months he spent in a mental institution after World War II, since he suffered from amnesia. But he remembered enough to write convincingly of the cruel ways patients were treated and of the absurd practices carried out in the hospital in both his novel and autobiography. Three poems in *Adventures of the Letter I* are derived, in one way or another, from his experiences in the institution: "Permission to Operate a Motor Vehicle," "Simplicity," and "Cynthia." The first draws upon incidents recorded in *Riverside Drive;* the second is a sympathic study of an institutionalized woman; and the third is a brief portrait of a woman who is not in an institution but who because of an abortion and an irrational fear of the Mafia is quite disturbed.

There are other poems in *Adventures of the Letter I,* such as "An American Peasant" and "Port Jefferson," that can be classed as personal. And there are naturally other subject areas over the years that Simpson has taken on but which have not been touched on in this chapter, primarily because they have not received his constant attention in the way war, love, America, and, recently, the personal have. Simpson's poems in *Adventures of the Letter I* are personal in a biographical sense. Those in his previous collections are, of course, personal, as Simpson has repeatedly said; but in the earlier poems, he manages to create a sense of character in the speakers—a character, in fact, who is indeed speaking for Simpson, but who possesses a personality of his own. Therefore, the personal sans mask is a relatively recent departure for Simpson. For William Stafford, the subject of our last chapter in this study, the personal has been a constant since the beginning.

4 William Stafford

WILLIAM STAFFORD'S poetic alliance with the makers of the Emotive Imagination is a unique and largely fortuitous one. He has never embraced unequivocally the method of the imagination as we have defined it here, though major versions of it appear in all his volumes. Nor has he totally abandoned traditional prosodic structures—even though experimentation in meter and rhyme has been constant. A significant number of Stafford's poems are written in free verse. He has never been strongly identified with the poetics of Robert Bly, though his work has received the commendation of Bly, Louis Simpson, Donald Hall, James Dickey, and others. Furthermore, short poems by Stafford demonstrating a poetry of surreal images which appeal to certain alogical associations appeared as early as the collection which made up his doctoral dissertation in 1954. Poems by Stafford employing qualities of the Emotive Imagination are therefore important, not only because they demonstrate an independence and individuality in the emergence of the new poetry, but also because they rank among the finest lyrics written in America in the past two decades.

Stafford has published more poems than any of the other three poets considered here; he is also the oldest (born in 1914), though he came to the serious writing of poetry relatively late.

One would not speak of the emergence of Stafford's poetry so much from the Imagist-Projectivist tradition as from that of the Transcendentalists and Robert Frost.

Both in metrics and in theme, the poems of William Stafford are relatively consistent. The poet was forty years old when he submitted a collection of thirty-five short poems as his doctoral dissertation at the State University of Iowa under the title *Winterward*. This group, largely unknown, was drawn upon for succeeding volumes. With the publication of *West of Your City* in 1960 Stafford reprinted four poems from *Winterward* identically and three others with only minor modifications. "Elegy" was reprinted with slight alterations in *Traveling through the Dark* in 1962. His 1966 volume *The Rescued Year* printed one poem identically from the dissertation and three others slightly revised. The juxtaposition of almost any poem from *West of Your City* with one from the 1973 volume *Someday, Maybe,* for example, would not evince startling differences in style or themes.

Stafford's poems reveal thematically a singular and unified preoccupation. The voice of his work speaks from a sheltered vista of calm and steady deliberation. The speaker looks backward to a western childhood world that is joyous and at times edenic, even as he gazes with suspicion and some sense of peril upon the state of modern American society. The crux of each volume by Stafford involves the search for that earlier age identifiable by certain spiritual values associated with the wilderness, values which can sustain him and his family as well as the whole of the technological and urban society which surrounds him. The means to this search come through a poetry of images, images frequently and profoundly mythic. The investigation of these themes in the work of Stafford will constitute the discussion which follows. Before tracing them, however, one should be aware of the mode of the Emotive Imagination at work in Stafford's poetry and how it, specifically, contributes to the moral concerns of his work.

The setting of Stafford's poetry is western, ranging from Kansas, the state of his birth and boyhood, to Oregon, where he has taught for more than two decades. As a result, Stafford's outdoor world is a landscape of nature writ large: there is the wind of poems like "Tornado" and "Before the Big Storm" and the sky of "Holding the Sky." His preferred world is "The Farm on the Great Plains," as one poem has it, or "At Cove on the Crooked River." In almost every case, the descriptive imagery accompanying these poems discloses a deeply human value symbolically inherent in the landscape. It is, in short, a setting ideally suitable to the poetry of the Emotive Imagination and one markedly distinct from the more midwestern settings of Bly and Wright. If a lyric by Robert Bly is likely to be set in a snowy Minnesota corn field, for example, one by Stafford will be located on the side of a mountain or along a riverbank. The setting is partially accountable for a distinction in the tone of the given lyric. There is less of the soft effusiveness one is likely to find, for example, in a poem by James Wright. As Stafford says in "The Preacher at the Corner," "Unavoidable / hills have made me stern, determined not to be wavery." Another quality that forestalls the "waveryness" of Stafford's poetry is his relative adherence to regular and formal metrical and stanzaic patterns.

The qualities which Stafford shares with the other poets of the Emotive Imagination, however, are basic. Although the poem itself more often speaks through the first person plural in a Stafford poem than the first person singular, the poet's activity is often solitary. Stafford's use of the collective "we" universalizes his own experiences. While the drama underlying the poem may originate in the external world, it can dart inward with sharp abruptness. The inward propulsion of the poem also follows upon the juxtaposition of images. The state of silence in a given poem, essential to the poetics of Robert Bly, is prominent in two of Stafford's finest poems: "From the Gradual Grass" and "The Animal That Drank Up Sound." In the former, a poem Paul

Ramsey calls "one of the few great lyrics of this century," [1] it is a silence itself which emerges from the "gradual grass," portending a hopeful prospect in a world where "Walls are falling!" In the latter, an unidentified animal simply subsumes the sounds of nature:

> In all the wilderness around he
> drained the rustle from the leaves into the mountainside
> . . . .
> he buried—
> thousands of autumns deep—the noise that used to come there.

The poems of *West of Your City* (1960) are almost all written in colloquial diction but, even so, in fixed meters. They also depend heavily on images. A poem like "Vacation," discussed in Part I, Chapter 1, shows Stafford's mastery of the essential process of the Emotive Imagination. One could also point to "Hail Mary," "Lore," "Weather Report," "The Well Rising," and especially "Two Evenings" as examples of Stafford's serious experimentation with the juxtaposition of images in semisurrealist constructions. The narrative background is minimal in these examples; images gather and meaning inheres in their accumulation.

Traveling through the Dark (1962) reveals a greater commitment to a poetry that makes its pitch not so much to logical continuity in narration as to unconscious association through images. The volume also discloses Stafford's first elaborate use of free verse. "Universe Is One Place," a minor poem, displays openly the new looseness. The poem begins:

> Crisis they call it?—when
> when the gentle wheat leans at the combine and
> and the farm girl brings cool jugs wrapped in burlap
> slapping at her legs?

1. Paul Ramsey, "What the Light Struck," *Tennessee Poetry Journal,* II (Spring, 1969), 19.

The question of line 1 is answered through the images of the question in lines 2–4. The poem's principal punctuation is that of the question mark and dash, opening up the structure. Repetition of words from the end of one line to the beginning of the next undercuts more conventional, logical connectives. Personification of certain images ("the gentle wheat leans") is strongly reminiscent of Bly and Wright. The final response to the "crisis" of line 1 is contained in the poem's concluding line, a line which defies syntactical, though not imagistic, clarity: "City folks make / Make such a stir. / Farm girl away through the wheat."

Stafford has alluded briefly to this method which relies more upon syllabic content than full rhymes or regular meter: "Instead of assuming that the language has syllables with many sounds, only certain ones matched for rhyme or equivalent duration or emphasis, I assume that all syllables rhyme, sort of. That is, any syllable sounds more like any other syllable than it sounds like silence. . . . Once the writer accepts this total relation to the language, most discussions about meter and form (in regard to sound) become inadequate."[2] In the first stanza of "Universe Is One Place" quoted above, there are no full rhymes among the terminal syllables of any lines. There are, of course, the total rhymes involved in the repetition of "when / when" as well as "and / and." Equally important, however, Stafford's open and loose syntax invites more subtle syllabic echoes: the vocalic rhyme of "wheat leans," the proximate rhyme of "wrapped" and "slapping," the consonant rhyme of "jugs" and "legs." This mode of "syllabic rhyme," as Stafford calls it, eschews the obvious and inevitable rhyme, one which would distract from the quiet flow of the images. Conversely, the more hidden rhymes actually enhance the psychic play of the same images.

Since *Traveling through the Dark,* each of Stafford's succeed-

2. William E. Stafford, "Finding the Language," in Stephen Berg and Robert Mezey (eds.), *Naked Poetry* (New York: The Bobbs-Merrill Co., 1969), 82.

ing volumes has contained poems similar in method to "Universe Is One Place." *The Rescued Year* in 1966 reprinted early poems from *West of Your City* like "Vacation" and "The Well Rising" and included new poems such as "Across Kansas" and "Right Now"—all of which draw upon a procession of images which culminate in disclosing a state of the unconscious. *Weather,* a private 1969 collection, continues the practice, especially in a poem like "When We Got to Chitina." Again in *Allegiances,* 1970, poems of the Emotive Imagination are present. "In Fog," one of the more memorable, is quoted here in entirety:

> In fog a tree steps back.
>
> Once gone, it joins those hordes
> blizzards rage for over tundra.
>
> With new respect I tell
> my dreams to grant all claims;
>
> Lavishly, my eyes close between
> what they saw and that far flood
>
> Inside: the universe that happens
> deep and steadily.

The title of the poem, coupled with the dream of the poem's speaker, introduces the reader to a surreal world where boundaries of ordinary perception are blurred. The poem also illustrates the particular metaphoric quality of the Emotive Imagination. The tree's envelopment in fog identifies with the speaker's dream and its recession into "that far flood / Inside." The two phenomena, the trees and the dream, otherwise seem to have little in common. They are, however, related by their absorption in uncontrollable weather. The fog-bound tree joins "those hordes / blizzards rage for over tundra." Similarly, the dream is divided by the "far flood / Inside." The two elements of the metaphor coalesce fully when the "blizzards" without and the "flood" within are brought to tranquillity by the poem's concluding statement: "The universe that happens / deep and steadily."

That which was distinctly personal becomes general and accessible to the reader's own experience. Even the tree, perhaps the most objective element of the poem, is personified into the subjective: "In fog a tree steps back." The poem's first line consequently encapsulates the movement of the Emotive Imagination. As the real is rendered surreal, the fog merges with the dream. At the end, both images unite in the general. It is the images, in any case, which propel the reader inward; the poem stops at the instant of recognition. Stafford employs similar processes in other poems from *Allegiances,* especially "Stories from Kansas" and "What I Heard Whispered at the Edge of Liberal, Kansas."

"Owl," from *Someday, Maybe,* (1973) presents a winter setting, within which are juxtaposed an owl, a snowflake, the stars, and extinct tribes of men. In the third stanza, each image links up with the others, and ultimately with the fate of all men, in the proclamation of evanescence and mortality:

> No witness but the eyes,
> no flake at large but wings,
> no sound but the flow of stars,
> and a claw of moon
>   in the wood.

Another poem from the same volume, "Dreams To Have," situates images as frames on a strip of film or painting in a gallery, images which arrest the flux of time, but also epitomize it: "I remember that place / the rest of my life."

"Universe Is One Place," "In Fog," and "Owl" are poems which recall the achievements of Bly and Wright; they are not, however, representative in the larger sense of Stafford's own work. Many of his poems are not markedly surrealistic; most are not as prosodically loose as these poems. Furthermore, while these are essentially without narrative plot, most of Stafford's poems adhere rather closely to some narrative substructure; as he asserts in "An Introduction to Some Poems," "we have to live that dream into stories."

Stafford's affinities with and contribution to the poetry of the
Emotive Imagination are perhaps more general, involving both
theme and technique. In its larger context, his poetry is essentially Janus-faced: it looks back with nostalgia upon an idealized
childhood, but never at a removal from a far more foreboding
perspective of modern society. His poetry seeks to chart the connectives between these two worlds. What, then, is the relation
between such a thematic preoccupation and the Emotive Imagination? It is precisely in the way by which the poetic imagination
seeks to link up the two perspectives. The childhood world is
extolled through images of the wilderness; the validity of that
world and the accessibility of its values are revealed through a
poetry of distinctly archetypal images. If "the rescued year" is
indeed recoverable, it will inevitably be found "west of your city."
In "Watching the Jet Planes Dive," Stafford exclaims, "We must
find something forgotten by everyone alive, / and make some fab-
ulous gesture."

Perhaps William Stafford is equaled only by Theodore
Roethke among American poets who cherish the memory of
childhood. Stafford goes beyond even Roethke, however, in defining the father as the central occupant of that near-perfect
world. If for Dylan Thomas the childhood eden of "Fern Hill"
finds him "honoured among foxes and pheasants" and "prince of
the apple towns," Stafford's eden is appreciably simpler: "Plain
black hats rode the thoughts that made our code." The Kansas
boyhood of Stafford, marking an epoch of American life between
the two wars, is rural, austere, inhabited by companionable
neighbors and dominated by family. Its value for Stafford,
though, is more than sentimental. It ultimately represents a way
of life that forcibly contradicts the urban world of the 1960s and
'70s. Its moral precepts derive directly from an intimate familiarity with the land and the wilderness: "... we ran toward
storms. / Wherever we looked the land would hold us up."

The nature of that plain childhood world provides a key to

Stafford's own attitude, one that shuns the fanciful in favor of the ordinary. In a brief comment on his poem "The Farm on the Great Plains," Stafford has acknowledged the presence of a "moral commitment mixed with a deliberate—even a flaunted—nonsophistication."[3] The occasional weakness of some of these poems occurs precisely when nonsophistication succumbs to the trite ("There was popcorn on the stove, / and her mother recalled the old days, inviting me back.") Stafford's nonsophistication is "flaunted," one suspects, to avoid the slightest trace of the meretricious or the mannered; in this attempt he has been successful. There is a kind of *Winesburg, Ohio* quality to these poems, an attempt to capture a whole family, a whole town. Even the titles suggest it: "The Preacher at the Corner," "The Girl Engaged to the Boy Who Died." However, if George Willard seeks to escape the small town at the end, William Stafford desperately tries to recover it.

In some poems Stafford casts the vision of his youth through mythic characters and settings. "In Medias Res," for example, is a poem whose title points to the epic conventions which underlie its statement. Possibly as a dream, the first stanza situates the poet on the streets of a town at night surrounded by his father and his son. The unity of the generations through the love of the poet sends out the mythic spell: "There was a one-stride god on Main that night, / all walkers in a cloud." The power of the familial bond ignites the setting of the poem so that the town becomes the conflagration of Troy. It concludes in an outcry: "'Aeneas!' I cried, 'just man, defender!' / And our town burned and burned." In other poems similar mythic contexts, all with overtones of the golden age, are invoked. "At Liberty School," for example, reproduces the school-boy world and the emotional power of the "Girl in the front row who had no mother." (Stafford lived one year in

3. William E. Stafford in Paul Engle and Joseph Langland (eds.), *Poet's Choice* (New York: Dell Publishing Co., 1962), 143.

Liberal, Kansas, and graduated from Liberal High School.) The mounting force of the poet's memory of the girl transforms the poem in the fourth stanza into the heroic utopia of Atlantis. The images are characteristic of the Emotive Imagination:

> Our town now is Atlantis, crystal-water bound;
> at the door of the schoolhouse fish are swimming round;
> thinking in and out of the church tower go deep waves.

Another poem, "Twelve Years Old," reenacts an episode from the poet's childhood; the principal allusion is indirect, but it draws upon the promise of the land of milk and honey given to Moses and the exiled Jews. The twelve-year-old boy and his companions "found / honey in an old tree." The loss of that childhood is accompanied by the dissipation of the promised land:

> Far to a land all curved and green,
> a place the wind blew from,
> a poured-out land all honey smooth—
> a land that never did come.

In "That Weather," Stafford recasts the untroubled world of childhood in the life of his own son Bret, "a millionaire / of days he would never lose." It is, as Stafford says in the poem's last lines, a veritable golden age:

> These few lines record that time,
> for the annals of the world. There are such
> golden things, and all the rest is about them.
> Rome rose, and fell, for these.

From Virgil to Exodus, from Atlantis to Rome, Stafford's nostalgia for his youth on the plains of the American midwest is mythically shaped. There is a certain irony in these allusions, however; the appeal of that childhood world is deliberately unheroic in its outward activity. Its memory is precious for the very fact that it is undramatic.

Occasionally, the mythic transformation of Stafford's childhood is less literary and more atavistic: "We were a people together / alive in the bush again," in "Folk Song." "In the Old Days" revolves around the memory of the mother's stories of "the wide field" which surrounds the home, a field occupied by "strange animals" who approach the house and call out to its inhabitants: "Then Mother sang. But we listened, beyond: / we knew that the night she had put into a story was real." In both instances, the focus is not so much on family as on the land itself. If Stafford's poetry is religious or mystical in its response to the wilderness, that impulse emerges not only from the Bible but from the natural world: "Around our home were such tall legends, / everything carved by winds and rivers."

The mythic quality of the childhood world is dominated by the figure of the father who appears in dozens of Stafford's poems. Earl Ingersoll Stafford worked for Bell Telephone and K-T Oil Company before his death in 1942. These positions caused the Stafford family to move about throughout Kansas—though Stafford himself lived in Hutchinson, Kansas, the town of his birth, for all but three or four years before his graduation from high school in Liberty, Kansas. In these poems the father is always regarded from the point of view of the son who has survived him, but who continues to look to him as preceptor and guide. In a private letter Stafford acknowledges, "My father did in fact represent a fervent and sustaining influence. When I read of others who find themselves rebelling against their fathers and so on, I have to use my imagination."[4] The father who appears in the poems is heroic: he is provider and protector; his moral strength is steady and independent of worldly expectations; most important of all, he is the high priest of the wilderness. Like Sam Fathers to Isaac McCaslin or Natty Bumppo to the neophytes of the frontier, Stafford's father is initiator and instructor to the son, not only in relation to the wilderness itself, but in the moral values which inhere within it. Again like Fathers and Leatherstocking,

4. Stafford to George Lensing, July 15, 1972.

he is imbued with certain mystical, almost superhuman, powers. An early poem, "Listening," exalts the father's prowess in perceiving the steps of animals or the moths against the screen: "we would watch him look up and his face go keen / till the walls of the world flared, widened." A visionary power is attributed to him in "The Swerve" where his ability to drive across a bridge at night after the car "went blind" derives from "a light he kept in mind." In "The Rescued Year" the father is described in religious terms and is given a vision of prophetic magnitude. The poem recounts the church-going of Stafford's youth, the response to which, on the father's part, is "mean." He then recalls the rides home from church:

> —and going home his wonderfully level gaze
> would hold the state I liked, where little happened
> and much was understood. I watched my father's finger
> mark off huge eye-scans of what happened in the creed.

The figure of the father in these poems occasionally assumes the archetypal dimensions of the universal father. One of the titles, "Parentage," suggests this enlargement from the individual to the universal. Under the general title "Following the *Markings* of Dag Hammarskjöld: A Gathering of Poems in the Spirit of His Life and Writings" appears another of these poems, again implying the extension of the father beyond the individual. The psychological ramifications of this relationship between son and father consequently take on a general application, one which lends itself, perhaps not consciously on Stafford's part, to specific Freudian and Jungian illustrations. The correspondences between the father as he appears in the poetry and certain analytical psychologies remain partial and tentative; but to the degree that the figure transcends the individual in the universal, such systems can be insightful.

The Oedipal pattern in the father-son relation is clearest in "Some Shadows," a poem which celebrates the gentle reserve and fragility of Stafford's mother: "A lean man, a cruel, took her. / I am his son." But if the father of this poem is in any sense a tyrant in the Freudian scheme, he is quickly recast in the ideal. [5]

The heroic pattern of the father's life serves as a model for the aspirant son, but ultimately it is unattainable. The function of the father according to this scheme unfolds in "Parentage." Here he is remembered as alienated from society, so strong in himself as to be self-sufficient, though to the world "he was over-whelmed." The son cannot model himself upon such a measure, preferring "to be saved and not, like him, heroic." The conclusion, one which is contradicted in other poems, is the relief of dissociation: "I want to be as afraid as the teeth are big, / I want to be as dumb as the wise are wrong: / I'd just as soon be pushed by events to where I belong."

The ambivalence of the son is revealed in another poem from the same volume, *Traveling through the Dark*. In "Elegy" the opposite of dissociation is desired—even though again the activity of the father is heroic, here cosmic:

> At sight of angels or anything unusual
> you are to mark the spot with a cross,
> for I have set out to follow you
> and these marked places are expected,
> but in between I can hear no sound.

The presence of the father is manifest in Stafford's poetry according to a variety of psychological tensions: association/disassocia-

---

5. *Totem and Taboo,* one of Freud's most anthropological studies, speaks of the pattern by which the despised father, following his desired death, is exalted: "The ambivalent attitude towards the father has found a plastic expression in it, and so, too, has the victory of the son's affectionate emotions over his hostile ones. The scene of the father's vanquishment, of his greatest defeat, has become the stuff for the representation of his supreme triumph. The importance which is everywhere, without exception, ascribed to sacrifice lies in the fact that it offers satisfaction to the father for the outrage inflicted on him in the same act in which that deed is commemorated." *Totem and Taboo,* trans. James Strachey (New York: W. W. Norton and Co., 1950), 149–50. It should be pointed out, however, that at no point do Stafford's poems explicitly entertain a death wish for the father. He has said elsewhere, "My father was far from oppressive." Letter to George Lensing, July 15, 1972.

tion; cruelty/love; success/failure—and underlying is a sense of continuing awe.

In one poem, "Some Shadows," Stafford honors the memory of both his parents in terms of the forces they continue to hold over him. The shadow itself is an image commonly enough associated with the dead. Carl Jung, however, defines the shadow as a major archetype latent in the unconscious: "The conscious mind is on top, the shadow underneath, and just as high always longs for low and hot for cold, so all consciousness, perhaps without being aware of it, seeks its unconscious opposite." [6] From this perspective one might also regard the pressing memory of parents, partially conscious, partially unconscious, as Jungian: "Forgive me these shadows I cling to, good people." Another poem, "Shadows," which appeared in the Spring, 1970, issue of *Field,* is archetypal. It includes the setting of boyhood: "There is a place in the air where / our old house used to be." The poem goes on to define Jung's "shadow life":

> At a fountain on Main Street I saw
> our shadow. It did not drink but
> waited on cement and water while I drank.
> There were two people and but one shadow.
> I looked up so hard outward that a bird
> flying past made a shadow on the sky.

Jung's discussion of the father insists that the son's "imago" of the father is conditioned by the image of the son's own unconscious. The father is never imaged as he objectively exists, but as a "compound" containing the specific reactions of the child. The "imago" is therefore both subjective and objective. In "The Relation between the Ego and the Unconscious," Jung describes the effect of the "imago" upon the son after the father's death: "The image is unconsciously projected, and when the parents die, the

6. C. G. Jung, "On the Psychology of the Unconscious," in *Two Essays on Analytical Psychology* (New York: 1953), 64.

projected image goes on working as though it were a spirit existing on its own. The primitive then speaks of parental spirits who return by night (revenants), while the modern man calls it a father or mother complex." [7] The father as revenant, a projection of the son's own unconscious memory, is not uncommon in these poems. One can see the manner in which the Jungian spirit-vision corresponds to the process of the Emotive Imagination. Images fix upon the external world; they evoke, however, an appearance or revelation which is interior. Objective phenomena summon the psychic vision. "Fall Journey" operates as a poem according to this pattern:

> Evening came, a paw, to the gray hut by the river.
> Pushing the door with a stick, I opened it.
> Only a long walk had brought me there,
> steps into the continents they had placed before me.
>
> I read weathered log, stone fireplace, broken chair,
> the dead grass outside under the cottonwood tree—
> and it all stared back. We've met before, my memory
> started to say, somewhere. . . .
>
> And then I stopped: my father's eyes were gray.

The final line, in gathering the other images of gray in the poem, dramatically reveals the "imago" of the spirit-father. In another context Stafford has spoken of the role which memory of the father plays in the actual writing of poems: "I sometimes find myself thinking of a phrasing and then ascribing it to him in a poem—but there is a certain kind of justice in that, as I come close to thinking that he continues to say things!" [8]

The specific moral influence of Stafford's father is of course less universal and more personal. Through all these poems he emerges as the man at peace with himself and the world. In "Father's Voice," this is his bequest to his son: "He wanted me to

---

7. C. G. Jung, "The Relations Between the Ego and the Unconscious," *ibid.*, 196.
8. Stafford to George Lensing, July 15, 1972.

be rich / the only way we could, / easy with what we had." In a highly personal way, Stafford's own pacifism seems to have found a precedent in his father.[9] But the poet is sparing in specific details, a fact which reinforces the universality of the figure.

Another character-type who corresponds to the father in the poetry of Stafford is the American Indian. Like the father, the Indians and their chiefs are dead; and their wisdom also derives from intimacy with the wilderness. They too impart their wisdom, heroically purchased, to their survivors through the agency of the poem. "Boone Children," from *Weather,* presents the Indians, here Shawnees, as aged figures who speak to the "children." The chief acquiesces paternally in the request of the children for passage through the territory. He then "went back into the leaves. The poem concludes,

> Today we might find that chief, and the right thing
> might get said, till the calendar moaned away through
> the trees, as the Boone children said yes.

The rediscovery of the lost chief whose prophetic counsel might yet prevail is the subject of many of the Indian poems. The barriers of time are dissolved ("the calendar moaned away").

The qualities by which the Indian is most consistently defined are not ferocity and warfare, but reticence and concealment, an insight common to the Indian poems of both Wright and Simpson. His life is enacted according to rituals and symbolic patterns which bring him into harmony with the wilderness. He is marked by his withdrawal, both imposed and preferred, from the predator-settlers. In "The Concealment: Ishi, the Last Wild Indian," Ishi is defined as "the shadow man" whose survival depends upon hiding. He fails and with his death the mythic ritual of Indian life also dissolves: "Erased / footprints, berries that purify the breath, rituals / before dawn with water." In

9. See "A Farewell Picture" from *Weather* (Mt. Horeb, Wis.: The Perishable Press, 1969).

"The Last Day," Ishi is replaced by Geronimo, another doomed figure whose final refuge is concealment. His extinction corresponds in the poem to Heraclitus' ascent from rocks to water to air: "To Geronimo rocks were the truth, / water less, air not at all; / but the opposite he had to learn."

Perhaps the two most successful Indian poems are from *Traveling through the Dark:* "A Stared Story" and "Returned to Say." The former is a sonnet where, in the octave, the Indians, upon returning to camp "feasted till dark in the lodge of their chief." They then rode away over the "earth their mother." The sestet suggests a contemporary reenactment of the earlier cyclical life of the Indians now gone: "Often at cutbacks where roots hold dirt together / survivors pause in the sunlight, quiet, pretending / that stared story. . . ." The "wild world" is momentarily recaptured, as the poem's last words prescribe, "by imagination."

"Returned to Say" is Stafford's most purely mythopoeic Indian poem. It describes a meeting between the speaker and "a lost Cree." Together, they embark upon an ancient journey which leads to the discovery of a "new vision." There are overtones of the medieval grail romance where the knight is met by a father-helper figure who leads the knight through a series of initiatory and purifying acts. The quest is defined by hardship: "It will be a long trip"; "he is to find a path." A series of sacramental acts must be performed before the disclosure of the looked-for "sign." In part, the activity is baptismal: "we have drunk new water from an unnamed stream." Even the breathing of the Cree is an act of consecration: "there is a grain of sand on his knifeblade / so small he blows it and while his breathing / darkens the steel his eyes become set." The "sign" turns out to be, not the holy grail, but the very activity of the journey itself: "We will mean what he does." And the poem's final irony is contained in the idea that, while the journey involves the physical world of the wilderness, its reality is spiritual: "Our moccasins do not mark the ground." The poem illustrates a tenet which underlies all of Stafford's Indian poems:

most of the Indians have been violently removed;[10] their pattern
of life, adherent to the values of the wilderness, remains a richly
attractive alternative to contemporary society. In this sense, the
lost Cree, the Shawnees, Ishi, Geronimo, Crazy Horse, and the
rest have "returned to say."

The childhood world, for all its mythic import, is past, and
"the rescued year" is saved from oblivion only through the language of poetry. Family and friends of youth have departed; the
Indian civilizations of the past are reduced to captive feebleness.
The values by which that lost world existed, however, remain
possible; they are indeed a desperately prescribed remedy in the
face of perils which Stafford sees on every side. The nature of
those perils occupies a major portion of Stafford's canon as a poet.
The precarious world in which the poet finds himself is described
through three principal categories. The first is composed of the
dangers of the wilderness and nature itself, dangers that existed
as much in the past as in the present, though they seem more
acute now. The second category is made up of specific descrip-
tions of modern, technological society. The poems here are concerned with the threats of nuclear war, of a ravaging industrial
society, and of a mechanical existence that divorces the individual from authentic human values. Finally, some poems form a
category which exposes the sham and vapidity of modern social
behavior.

It is important to note that in the last two instances Stafford is
presenting the reader with an impression of modern society that
is diametrically opposed to the idealized world of childhood. The
two worlds, in fact, stand almost irreconcilably apart. Finally, it
is the vocation of the poet to discover the means by which the two
poles can be brought together so that modern society can be
redeemed. That will only occur, however, by the unequivocal

---

10. See "In the Oregon Country" from *West of Your City* (Los Gatos, Calif.: The
Talisman Press, 1960).

embrace of the ethos which informed the life of the western boyhood of Stafford.

Although many of his poems suggest that Stafford's view of the childhood world is innocently utopian, this vision does not hold universally. The same resources of the wilderness which nourish the happiest human existence also disclose a kind of Darwinian struggle wherein predation and decay lurk. "With One Launched Look," "Chickens and Weasel Killed," "Love the Butcher Bird Lurks Everywhere" are poems which, as their titles suggest, betray the inhospitable in nature. A fundamental lesson of the nature world is that all life is defined by insecurity and transitoriness. "Winterward," for example, hints at the seasonal thrust of the year toward winter and death. The movement itself is beset with "threatenings":

> a foxfire of fear, the distrust
> of sighting under a willow tree
> a little eggshell, burst.

"Small Items" and "Things We Did that Meant Something" elaborate the same theme: nature falling over in winter and prefiguring the inevitable fall of the human observer. In such instances, "a fateful diagram" is the only acceptable reading of the world.

Persons who populate such a world are themselves marked victims. Their existence is so precarious that even the inhalation of the next breath of air is uncertain. "In the Cold" allegorically defines the abandoned astronaut locked outside his rocket on a hostile planet:

> And listen: the wind has come.
> Finally, it always does.
> It will touch everything.

As its title allegorizes, "A Human Condition" disabuses one of the security of home, farm, and forest; all "will indict." Even the wilderness and the land offer no permanent refuge: "These places could have been home, / are lost to you now. They are foreign but good."

Being alert and cautious affords some protection against the natural disasters of the world. In any case, human volition is relatively helpless in correcting the aberrances themselves. The same cannot be said for the more ominous threats that emerge in Stafford's verse. These are humanly invented and humanly imposed.

Of special concern to Stafford are those means of technology that endanger the wilderness. It is a theme to which he returns in every volume. "They have killed the river and built a dam," he asserts in "The Fish Counter at Bonneville." Oil well engines have outlasted the vigilance of the snakes in "Boom Town." Especially in "Quiet Town" the ironic silence and reserve of the community only thinly cover various acts of delinquency: "Technicians in suicide plan courses / in high school for as long as it takes." The automobile graveyard is taken as a symbol of contemporary standards for succeeding generations in "Time": "The river was choked with old Chevies and Fords. / And that was the day the world ended."

In poems such as these Stafford shares with Bly, Wright, and Simpson a distrust and disavowal of much of what he finds in modern society. Unlike these poets, however, Stafford's appraisal of that scene is not so much founded upon the disparity between the wealthy and the poor, or between unscrupulous capitalists and ostracized misfits. Rather, it is the rapacious destruction of the natural world, the environment of all men, that most perplexes him.

Perhaps most heinous of all is the threat of imminent nuclear annihilation. The presence of bomb testing sites and missile silos upon the plains of the wilderness elicits a particular horror. "Our City Is Guarded by Automatic Rockets" speaks of the "cornered cat," the rocket itself, which is "now ready to spend / all there is left of the wilderness, embracing / its blood." A similar imagistic setting occurs in "At the Bomb Testing Site," a poem which Bly includes in his *Forty Poems Touching on Recent American History*. Here, a lizard braces itself for existence in a world which has become a desert, "a continent without much on it." Less apocalyptically, "Evening News" fixes on the nighly ritual of hearing war reports, presumably those from Vietnam, as they are broadcast over television (". . . a war happens, / only an eighth of an inch thick."). The poet's recourse is to immerse himself, somewhat desperately, in the surroundings of his own life, to which he addresses a prayer:

> In the yard I pray birds,
> wind, unscheduled grass,
> that they please help to make
> everything go deep again.

As victim of the holocaust in "The Whole Story," the poet is subsumed by leaves, sky, and winter through which he reaches out toward the children-survivors.

Stafford's dismay at the war in Indo-China is neither faddish nor a pose. During the years of World War II (Stafford was twenty-seven in 1941), he was a conscientious objector who served in several Civilian Public Service camps for religious objectors in Arkansas and California. A collection of essays describing various work details, friends he made in the alternate service, and the hostility he encountered during these years was published in 1947 under the title *Down in My Heart*. [11] Stafford has indicated that his deferment was technically granted on religious grounds, though his objection was not purely sectarian: "I was more a social objector, with benevolence but no firm doctrinal bent." [12] Stafford's introductory essay to *The Achievement of Brother Antoninus* takes note of the San Francisco poet's refusal to

---

11. A third printing of *Down in My Heart* in a paperback edition was issued in 1971 from The Brethren Press, Elgin, Illinois.

12. Stafford to George Lensing, July 31, 1972.

serve in the armed forces in World War II; the description of that poet's response to war and "political turmoil" might apply to much of Stafford's own work: "Pressures in the long development spring from the distinguishing issues of our time—World War II, the moral crises incident to war and the uprootings that go with it, the political turmoil felt by a whole alienated group, and the emotional revulsions of a conscientious and sensitive human being subjected to such pressures."[13]

"Traveling through the Dark" is probably Stafford's most popular and frequently anthologized single poem. In its broadest outline it reiterates the theme of confrontation between technology and wilderness, one which leads to the jeopardy of the latter. The poem is a narrative description of the poet's sojourn along a road at night leading to his discovery of a doe, victim of an earlier collision with another automobile. In a different context, Stafford has recalled the origin of the poem in a personal episode: "The poem concerns my finding a dead deer on the highway. This grew out of an actual experience of coming around a bend on the Wilson River Road near Jordan Creek in Oregon, and finding this deer, dead. As I was recounting the story to my kids the next day, I discovered by the expressions on their faces that I was arriving at some area of enhancement in the narrative."[14] The poet's crisis of discovery is rendered even more acute by his sudden recognition of the unborn fawn: "her fawn lay there waiting, / alive, still, never to be born." As a result, he is thrust, both literally and symbolically, between the vulnerable world of the wilderness represented by the doe and the predatory world of technocracy represented by his own automobile. The moral dilemma consequently is transferred to him: "I thought hard for us

13. William E. Stafford, "Brother Antoninus—The World as a Metaphor" in *The Achievement of Brother Antoninus* (Glenview, Ill.: Scott, Foresman and Company, 1967), 3.

14. Philip L. Gerber and Robert J. Gemmett, "Keeping the Lines Wet: A Conversation with William Stafford," *Prairie Schooner,* XLIV (Summer, 1970), 132.

all." In its outward sense, the decision is an obvious and easy one. The dead doe and the unborn fawn must be removed from the path of traffic: "It is usually best to roll them into the canyon: / that road is narrow; to swerve might make more dead." This he finally elects to do. The poet's removal of the obstacle, however, is attended with irony and, through the images of the poem, a sense of self-incrimination. As he hesitates in making the decision about what to do with the doe, "my only swerving," he becomes aware of his personal relation to the animal and the larger life of which she is a part: "I could hear the wilderness listen."

The poem's imagery alone, without further obtrusive commentary, defines his personal moral stance. The doe is "almost cold," while "her side was warm" with the life of the unborn fawn. The imagery of coldness-warmth is ironically inverted through the description of the automobile in which the poet himself, innocent of the actual killing, has been driving. He sees the victim "By glow of the tail-light." The car "aimed ahead its lowered parking lights." Even the poet stands "in the glare of the warm exhaust turning red." The life of the wilderness is ironically replaced in this manner by the life of the car. The poet's self-indictment emerges through his obvious identity with both worlds. He is able to abdicate neither. Furthermore, both worlds are presented in terms of life that suggest the human. The wilderness "listens," even as the car sinisterly has "aimed ahead its lowered parking lights," during which time the "steady engine" has "purred." Personifications bring home the fact that, while neither phenomenon is itself human, both are influences on human values.

"Traveling through the Dark" recalls the Emotive Imagination through its use of personifications and images. The images, however, are not surreal, and the poem itself remains consistently an objective narration. Stafford structures the poem upon four four-line stanzas and a concluding couplet. Irregular in meter, the poem employs no regular rhyme scheme—only occasional half-rhymes: "road / dead," "canyon / reason," "engine / listen." In its formal aspects, the poem is characterized by its economy of statement. Its easy colloquialism camouflages to a degree this organization. As Charles F. Greiner has pointed out, the use of a single word can be significant. The unborn fawn is described as "alive, still, never to be born." The word "still" sustains meanings on at least three levels: (1) still as *yet* alive; (2) still as *quiet,* indeed, so silent he hears "the wilderness listen"; (3) still as "stillborn," an inevitable association with the appearance of both "still" and "born" within the same phrase. [15]

"Traveling through the Dark" defines in trenchant terms the invasion of the wilderness by a new civilization. At times, as other poems express, the poet is forced, more directly than through the use of an automobile, to intercept that world. Stafford himself has not lived in isolation outside modern social environments. Like Wright and Simpson, he holds a Ph.D., having studied at the State University of Iowa. He has been affiliated with the teaching of literature at various universities for more than twenty-five years. As poetry consultant to the Library of Congress, he lived in Washington, D.C., in 1970/71, and has traveled extensively around the United States giving poetry readings. While he is no stranger to modern society, Stafford's poems leave little doubt that his allegiances belong to the untamed, natural world of the West. One poem, "The Trip," describes a visit by the poet to a drive-in restaurant, the whole of that episode enveloped in the artificial and dehumanizing: "A waitress with eyes made up to be Eyes / brought food spiced by the neon light." This impersonal world is characterized as "hollow on the outside, some kind of solid veneer." In "Have You Heard This One?" a stewardess on an airplane has "forged her face" cosmetically. She meets a passenger who asks, " 'Haven't I seen / you everyplace before?' " They marry "that very night in a

---

15. Charles F. Grenier, "Stafford's 'Traveling through the Dark': A Discussion of Style," *English Journal,* LV (November, 1966), 1018.

motel." The poem ends, "This is a true story. / It happened in New York / and Los Angeles / and Chicago / and . . . ." Other poems evince further the attempt by Stafford to shun the artificial world. "At the Chairman's Housewarming," for example, speaks of the banal conversation at a party where the talk is "like a jellyfish" in its course of idle banter. The poet does not absolve himself from this world and its conversation, but he implores at the end of the poem: "let me live definite, shock by shock." As a credo of his own poetics, Stafford proclaims in "An Introduction to Some Poems" that the individual and the poem pursue the same end: "The authentic . . . holds / together something more than the world, / this line."

Stafford's best poem on the artificiality of modern life is "A Documentary from America." It recounts a visit to a political rally where a presidential candidate is speaking. The rally is followed by the viewing of that event on a television report later in the day. The entire experience suggests manipulation and contrivance. The candidate's speech is "written by a committee"; the participants at the rally find that the television coverage makes them into unwitting supporters. As the poet witnesses the rally later on television, he is interrupted by yet another reporter:

> "Oh God," we said, "we were watching
> us, watching us." And in a terrible voice he roared,
> "Quick, be smiling; you are on the air again!" and—
> a terrible thing—we said just as he said, "How do you do."

The poetry of Stafford has been thematically examined up to this point in terms of two poles. The first is the idealized world of childhood upon the western plains of America in the earlier part of the twentieth century. It is dominated by the figure of the father and, by extension, the earlier Indian chieftains. This world is evanescent and exists principally through nostalgia, or, as Stafford says in "A Stared Story," "by imagination." The second pole fixes firmly upon the present world which surrounds

Stafford's adult life. It is seen almost exclusively in terms of fretful risk. The mechanized state of modern society which has forced the removal of man from his intimate identity with the land and nature is not only a threat to the continuation of the wilderness itself but insidiously reduces the terms of human existence to debilitating distortions and artificialities.

There is finally, however, a third state in the poetry of Stafford which is posited upon the kind of life the poet has attempted to stake for himself and his family. It is to some degree a romantic world which entails, necessarily, a partial retreat from the other and larger society which encloses him. But as a world of retreat it is not one of illusion. In the final analysis, the entire thrust of Stafford's work taken as a whole is toward the disclosure of a life that seeks to recapture the values of that other elusive and boyhood world. Consequently, these poems refuse to submit to the inflictions against the wilderness—both physical and spiritual. Rather, they are poems of desperate retrenchment.

The image in which Stafford casts himself in these poems is, to some extent, that of an isolated, sometimes lonely, advocate. Robert Creeley has spoken with some disapproval of Stafford's "wry wit, often, which can make peace with the complexities of times and places. . . . The danger is simply that things will become cozy ('The earth says have a place . . .'), and that each thing will be humanized to an impression of it merely."[16] It should be remembered, though, that Stafford's thematic conservatism in these poems does not emerge out of ignorance or insensitivity to the compelling issues of the larger world. To the contrary, he suggests that some form of retreat is finally the only remedy with which he can address those issues. The poems of what one might call the "modern wilderness" are calculated on Stafford's part to this end.

---

16. Robert Creeley, " 'Think What's Got Away,' " *Poetry,* CII (April, 1963), 44.

A major premise of these poems is that one's moral choices that lead to personal happiness depend integrally on the location of *where* one lives. Geography is the primary ingredient of personal gratification. In this sense, Stafford's poetry is as regionalist as that of southern poets like James Dickey. Many of the titles of poems suggest this regionalism: "West of Your City," "Walking West," "Across Kansas," "The Farm on the Great Plains," "Sunset: Southwest," "Stories from Kansas." All of these poems offer an alternative to an America where lives are marked by mobility, rootlessness, and insulation from the soil. Stafford is most overtly didactic on precisely this point: "One's duty: to find a place / that grows from his part of the world," or "The earth says have a place, be what that place / requires." A second criterion is a kind of burrowing in once the individual has found that location, a stubborn resolution to hold fast to one's chosen land. In "A Story," the poem's speaker observes mysterious climbers whose objectives are unknown: "they crawl far before they die." His own response is the opposite: "I make my hole the deepest one / this high on the mountainside." Another requirement is isolation. The secrets of the wilderness are divulged only to the one who removes himself from civilization. The "apparition river" of "By the Snake River" is lost when the poet "went / among the people to be one of them." Especially the spiritual life of nature is discernible only when "The railroad dies by a yellow depot, / town falls away toward a muddy creek." Finally, the fruits of the wilderness can never be discovered by rational chartings. "You thinkers, prisoners of what will work," are disavowed by Stafford in "An Epiphany" as he describes a brief and almost mystical encounter with a dog "in quick unthought." Such revelations are spontaneous, fleeting, and granted at moments when least expected.

The method of the Emotive Imagination is most apparent in the poems of the modern wilderness when Stafford seeks to define its concealed meanings. The deepest life of nature is revealed only rarely and under conditions outlined above. Even so, Stafford suggests an ambivalence in presenting the accessibility of those meanings. Glimpses (a favorite Stafford word) are possible; and, at times, a profound linking between the human and the nonhuman natural world occurs. On the other hand, Stafford occasionally suggests that the boundaries between the two worlds are impenetrable, and the imposition of the human is a tainting activity.

Stafford's depiction of the essential wilderness is set up through images—almost always in terms of a vertical hierarchy. The outer world is one of surfaces and shadows; it is available to everyone and yields many precious moments. The other world, concealed and far less accessible, is underground; its perception becomes the abiding vocation of the poet. "Bi-Focal" is one of the clearest definitions of the two separate dimensions of the wilderness:

> Love is of the earth only,
> the surface, a map of roads
> leading wherever go miles
> or little bushes nod.

> Not so the legend under,
> fixed, inexorable,
> deep as the darkest mine
> the thick rocks won't tell.

The "legend under" occupies the mythical gropings in this division of Stafford's verse. The imagistic arrangement of the concealed wilderness takes many forms, but almost always conforming to the vertical hierarchy. In "On the Glass Ice" it is the frozen fish under the surface over which the poet skates. In "Walking West" it is an underground badger: "Anyone with quiet pace who / walks a gray road in the West / may hear a badger underground." Here, "in deep flint another time is / caught." Corn planted by "starving Indians" of ancient generations can still be brought to harvest—*"that corn still lies"*—in "West of Your City." "In the Deep Channel," as the title suggests, is another account of revelation from under—here "a secret-headed channel cat." In moments of calm, the steadiness of life under the earth is sensed, as Stafford sets forth in "The Earth": "When the earth doesn't shake, when the sky / is still, we feel something under the earth: / a shock of steadiness." Although the truest reality of the wilderness is concealed below, its presence is manifest above. The opening stanza of "Weeds" attests to the irrepressible will of nature to "witness forth":

> What's down in the earth
> comes forth in cold water,
> in mist at night, in muttering
> volcanoes that ring oceans
> moving strangely at times.

One of Stafford's finest lyrics, "Connections," demonstrates again the vertical hierarchy of the wilderness life; it also summarizes the prerequisites for human perception of that life. The poem appeared originally in *West of Your City* and was selected by Stafford for republication in *The Rescued Year*:

> Ours is a low, curst, under-swamp land
> the raccoon puts his hand in,
> gazing through his mask for tendrils
> that will hold it all together.

> No touch can find that thread, it is too small.
> Sometimes we think we learn its course—
> through evidence no court allows
> a sneeze may glimpse us Paradise.

> But ways without a surface we can find
> flash through the mask only by surprise—
> a touch of mud, a raccoon smile.

> And if we purify the pond, the lilies die.

The several conditions for revelation of the concealed wilderness are all at work in this short lyric: its geographical setting is that of the poet's personal allotment in the wilderness ("Ours is a low, curst, under-swamp land"); it occurs in a remote and iso-

lated location as the poet clandestinely witnesses the activity of
the raccoon; the sought-after "glimpse" occurs "only by surprise"
and not by a rational process ("evidence no court allows").

"Connections" treats of two kinds of "surfaces" and two kinds
of under-surfaces in the wilderness life. As its title suggests, it is
an exploration of the linkings between the two levels. In the first
five lines of the poem, direct human activity is removed. The
raccoon itself stands over the surface of a pond and "puts his hand
in." The animal seeks a manifestation of the vital undersurface
life of the wilderness: "tendrils / that will hold it all together." He
fails, as line five explains. In the remainder of the poem, the
human pursuit of the same manifestation ensues. Again, "ways
without a surface" must be tried; the true vitality of the wilderness is concealed below. Here, the attempt is more successful and
occurs through deliberate irony. Like the raccoon, the human
cannot put his hand in to discover the "thread." In absolute terms
the boundaries between the two worlds are unbreachable. A
"glimpse," however, is possible, and this occurs through the
intercession of the raccoon itself. While the animal could not
itself "find that thread," it can become for the human perceiver a
mediator in the revelation of the wilderness. Accordingly, the
raccoon itself, an animal of the same untamed world, becomes an
extension of the same surface/undersurface division of the
wilderness. The face of the animal is twice described as a
"mask"—another surface that conceals the authentic life behind
it. The "touch of mud" and the "raccoon smile" become for the
human perceiver the instruments of revelation. The images of
the poem gather here to a climax of the Emotive Imagination. The
"under-swamp land" does reveal itself briefly but dramatically
through the smile of the raccoon, the removal of the mask. Irony
is crucial here: the swamp and the raccoon are finally one in that
the wilderness emanates from both. The human perceiver is
granted a miraculous insight into the world of nature, both
swamp and animal, through the raccoon's smile.

The poem concludes with an admonition: "And if we purify the pond, the lilies die." Human control can only be an ironic pollutant. The separation between human and wilderness life is absolute, and the latter claims its final autonomy.

The role of the raccoon in "Connections" is not unique. Animals are frequently invested with elevated positions in the life of the wilderness. The "comfortable earth" has excluded animal life, Stafford exclaims, in "Outside." Meanwhile, constantly encircling the periphery of human life is the coyote, ancient symbol of wisdom. The poem concludes with the suggestion that such wisdom can be reclaimed:

> For all we have taken into our keeping
> and polished with our hands belongs to a truth
> greater than ours, in the animals' keeping."

Similarly, the song of the sparrow in "In Response to a Question" or the singing of fish in "On the Glass Ice," become moral directives, as do deer tracks in "Deer Stolen." The idealized existence of animals is perhaps most comprehensively imparted in the poem "In Fur": "Owning the wilderness, they're not lost."

If "Connections" suggests that the unity between the wilderness and twentieth-century man is relative and fleeting, other poems pursue more positively that linking. "*Wild things wait,*" he insists in "West of Your City," and there are overlappings between the two worlds which suggest, at times, an almost mystical relationship. Asked about mysticism in his verse, Stafford does not deny it, although he insists that "I would like to be as clear and unambiguous as possible in my work." [17] Elsewhere, he has acknowledged "unanalyzed impressions of holiness" as a major theme in his work. [18] Occasionally, such as in a poem like "A

17. Gerber and Gemmett, "Keeping the Lines Wet: A Conversation with William Stafford," 128.
18. "Reciprocity vs. Suicide, Interview with William Stafford," *Trace*, XLVI (Summer, 1962), 223.

Walk in the Country," the description of the communion between poet and world seems spiritual in such a manner that the
experience approaches the purely religious:

> I felt a burden of silver come:
> my back had caught moonlight
> pouring through the trees like money.
>
> That walk was late, though.
> Late, I gently came into town,
> and a terrible thing had happened:
> the world, wide, unbearably bright,
> had leaped on me. I carried mountains.

Less prodigiously, other poems recognize instants of tangen-
tial mergings with nature that also appear sacramental. "Ceremony," for example, describes an episode where a muskrat bites
the finger of the poet while his hand is in the waters of the
Ninnescah River. His blood trails the current in the direction of
the ocean, effecting a momentary transformation of the wilderness "by a kind of marriage." A similar though more recent poem,
"Witness," acknowledges "the hand I dipped in the Missouri /
above Council Bluffs and found the springs." The hand, successful in its touch with the undersurface secret of the wilderness, becomes permanently blessed by the experience. These
poems of semimystical encounters with the natural world recall
those poems of James Dickey that center on fishing and hunting
outings. Stafford's, however, are less surrealistic and accompanied by calmer, deliberately less dazzling psychological effects
on the part of the speaker: "we study how to deserve / what has
already been given us."

In most of his work, Stafford's quest for the wilderness does
not seem aimed at portentous or mystical encounters. The western wilds, in fact, are niggardly in revealing their secrets to
human explorers. "A Survey" recounts the attempt to map the
area of the "Frantic Mountains," a mythological wilderness. The
"field boot crew" cannot even approach the area because of its

flooded rivers. Recalling the raccoon of "Connections," wildcats are then commissioned for a survey of their own kind, the only possible one, Stafford suggests. As we have seen, the wilderness does not altogether elude, though, and if the imposing conditions set forth by nature are met and if the perceiver will wait the "glimpses" and "surprises," he will not be totally impeded.

In most cases, the value in the actual pursuit of the unclaimed territories of nature is self-discovery—"to find / what I am," as he says in "By the Snake River." In the title poem of *Allegiances,* the making of oneself "sturdy for common things" as opposed to "strange mountains and creatures" is the most appealing human ambition. Finally, the wilderness remains the surest antidote for a world which, as we have seen in other poems, has run amuck in its misdirected course:

> "Some day, tame (therefore lost) men, the wild
> will come over the highest wall, waving
> its banner voice, beating its gifted fist:
> *Begin again, you tame ones; listen—the roads*
> *are your home again.*"

In the poems of the modern wilderness, Stafford again employs a form of myth,[19] but one which does not conform directly to patterns of earlier history or literature. He has, in fact, described these poems as a search for new myths:

I don't have any sense of larger purposes, just little immediate encounters. Beyond this, of course, aside from language there is a kind of resonance among our experiences. The key word might be *myth.* Every now and then we find ourselves encountering some story or pattern that wields more power over us than we would expect. I suppose that if I refer to the Oedipus story, we'll immediately have a reference point here. Someone, Sophocles or whoever, blundered into this pattern, and it has a lot of power. My assumption is that these patterns lie all around us. But as a writer it's too abrupt and cheap of me to think that my job is

---

19. See George S. Lensing, "William Stafford, Mythmaker," *Modern Poetry Studies,* VI (Spring, 1975), 1–17.

to take a pattern that Sophocles found and drape what I write around it. Instead of that, I would like to stumble on something new as Sophocles did. Of course, such patterns are rare, I realize.[20]

This "resonance among our experiences" almost always is rooted for Stafford in the location of the wilderness. In a private letter he has elaborated upon this setting of mythic investigation: "For me, myth comes at you in the way it did before it was formulated by anyone else. It comes from the influences on us all the time— gravity, wind, time, the immediacy of near things and the farness of far things—anything that touches you."[21]

Stafford's poetry does not give evidence of the attainment of a radically original and self-contained mythology. Indeed, many of the mythic patterns in his poems of the modern wilderness conform to fairly traditional romantic polarities: the superiority of the pastoral over the urban, the spontaneous over the rational, the isolated over the social. Even in more particularized versions of the wilderness certain traditional constructs are repeated. Stafford's play with mythic invention or modification occurs most noticeably when he seeks to establish some means of linking the human questor and the hidden wilderness. Some examples have already been witnessed, such as the raccoon's smile in "Connections" or the blood from the poet's finger in "Ceremony."

In a more traditional mythic framework some of the poems incorporate devices which seem almost inevitable in a poetry of this nature. As with the other poets of the Emotive Imagination, Stafford's exploration of the unconscious through the arrangement of images takes on certain primitive and archetypal impulses in some of the poems. "Reporting Back" from *Traveling through the Dark,* a short lyric of three couplets, hints at earlier forms of life which have been misplaced in the course of time.

20. Gerber and Gemmett, "Keeping the Lines Wet: A Conversation with William Stafford," 124–25.
21. Stafford to George Lensing, July 15, 1972.

The image of the lost path is central: "Is there a way to walk that living has obscured? / (Our feet are trying to remember some path we are walking toward.)" The quest of feet is replaced by the groping of hands in a notably similar poem, "Origins." More extensively, "From Eastern Oregon" depicts the typical removal from "the world's problem." In this case, the speaker enters a symbolic cave of ancient civilization where he reads "the carved story." The cave functions analogously to the path of "Reporting Back." The speaker himself goes on to assume an atavistic personality that leads him to "the swell of knowing":

> Your eyes an owl, your skin a new part of the earth,
> you let obsidian flakes in the dust discover your feet
> while somewhere drops of water tell a rock.

The cave of prehistoric life may be accessible symbolically, but its actuality is remote. For this reason, Stafford comes up short in comparison with a poet like Roethke, for example, in his recourse to primordial environments. The treasures of the wilderness can be poetically approached through real and contemporary measures. "In the Museum" presents objects from ancient and distant points, "a broken urn volcano-finished." Having viewed the various artifacts, the museum goer senses the impulse to identify with their origins—an impossible task, the poem implies. Instead, one fixes upon the present: "You never can get back, but there'll be other / talismans." Most of Stafford's modern wilderness poems investigate the nature of these "other talismans."

One would not wish to impose too stringently diagrammatic outlines upon Stafford's verse. The poems do not themselves conform to mechanical formulas. Yet, if the concealed wilderness and its essential vitality are presented beneath a variety of surfaces—below a river or underground, for example—the symbolic linkings between that part of the wilderness and its human perceiver are almost always presented as linear and horizontal. A vertical hierarchy functions in the various levels of the wilderness itself; a horizontal network describes the avenues between those levels and the poet's own person. This network consists of a variety of symbolic formulations, which also constitute a primary element in Stafford's mythological schema. Some, indeed, conform to traditional and archetypal associations. The journey is one example of this; the corridor is another.

We have already seen one illustration of the horizontal network in "Reporting Back," and that, of course, is the path. "Watching the Jet Planes Dive" is one of the poems where Stafford is most explicit in his discussion of the mythological overtones which emanate from the pursuit of the wilderness. Here, he advocates not the return to aboriginal sources, but to a forgotten past more intimately connected with the land. It is an activity that is "ritual" and one which entails the discovery of a "trail on the ground." Only such "wild beginnings" will counter the frenetic and eccentric patterns of modern life represented by the plunging of the jets overhead: "If roads are unconnected we must make a path, / no matter how far it is, or how lowly we arrive."

Closely related to the path is the more generalized notion of the journey itself. An inevitable motif in the search for the concealed wilderness, it is frequently incorporated in Stafford's verse. "Returned to Say" has already been considered as a kind of grail quest on the part of the poem's speaker and the lost Cree. The journey also informs, though less mythologically, the automobile passage of the poet in "Traveling through the Dark." In the lyric entitled "Journey" from *Someday, Maybe* human and animal life become a shared identity through the horizontal visual glance. The human perceiver ("You") encounters "a bear or / a wolf": "Eyes / give each other their flame and go out / when you meet."

The attractiveness of the journey motif to Stafford is partially attributable to its correspondence to earliest frontier life. The frontier journey by America's first explorers and settlers yielded the original and most fructifying manifestations of the unspoiled wilderness. "Boone Children" and "For the Grave of Daniel Boone" are two illustrations of this idealized journey. The latter recounts Boone's westward trek in terms of the construction of an ever-enlarging "home." Those of modern society who are Boone's "heirs" seek to repeat the same journey:

> Children, we live in a barbwire time
> but like to follow the old hands back—
> the ring in the light, the knuckle, the palm,
> all the way to Daniel Boone,
> hunting our own kind of deepening home.

The same journey is transferred to the poet himself in "Glimpses in the Woods." In this poem he describes a succession of yew trees deep within the woods, "giver of bows, drinker of shade." The poet allegorically defines "incidents of my journey" through this passageway and invites the reader to accompany him. The trees then provide a "corridor like a question, / a tunnel with one end, a mine meant / to escape from the dark." The column of trees symbolically serves both as an extension of the wilderness itself and a channel into its meaning, "the sacred blur." Another "twinned corridor" appears in "A Farewell Picture," one which extends from the poet's own eyes back to the war years of his youth and his father's steadfast resolution to shoot "only game with his rifle. / People, no."

Beyond the corridor, the trail, and the path—all of which contain the idea of journey—Stafford's other representations of the horizontal network are more surreal. Telephone wires, for example, have been a less conventional addition to this pattern. In "Long Distance," the sound of "ghostly voices" over the telephone elicits for the poet the prospect of overcoming time and returning to his youth and "the town back home."The same symbol informs "The Farm on the Great Plains" where the poet describes again his attempt to recover the idyllic life of his boyhood. Eventually, he speculates, "the line will be gone" and the meaning of his youth on the plains will be self-possessed:

> My self will be the plain,
> wise as winter is gray,
> pure as cold posts go
> pacing toward what I know.

The wire is further reduced to a ray of light in "Level Light," a poem that recalls Emily Dickinson's "There is a certain slant of light." In both poems a ray of afternoon sunlight signals the arrival of winter as a reminder of human mortality. Stafford's poem leads to the conclusion that failure in the eyes of the world, like the succumbing of afternoon and season, is the only manner of human progression.

Finally, a brief lyric of only eight lines, "Recoil," introduces the arrow dispatched from the bow. That burst of motion becomes metaphorically the poet's recollection as he seeks to "be myself again" by remembering home. The bow is appropriate to this act of moral release and recovery because it is a product of the wilderness, one that also remembers home:

> The bow bent remembers home long,
> the years of its tree, the whine
> of wind all night conditioning
> it, and its answer—Twang!

The images of the horizontal network have in common the fact that they are all representative of a psychological state: the reaching out of the human toward the wilderness—whether it be the modern wilderness, the wilderness of the poet's youth, or the wilderness of the American frontier. Each of these images— path, corridor, trail, tunnel, a visual glimpse, wire, ray of light, arrow—becomes a means of moral trajectory toward what is most authentic in human values; each represents what in "Found in a Storm" Stafford calls "meanings in search of a world."

The upshot of Stafford's poetry of the modern wilderness is a reaffirmation of American life in the twentieth century. It is true that poems like "At the Bomb Testing Site," "A Documentary from America," "Traveling through the Dark," and others remind us of the tenuous and imperiled state of that life. At times a meager stoicism seems the best resort: "Today we have to stand in absolute rain / and face whatever comes from God." Stafford's poetry epitomizes the quality of the Emotive Imagination—that for all its romanticism, this poetry will not take refuge in illusions or pretensions about the state of modern society. Part of his confidence in the future is founded upon the miraculous ability of the wilderness, independent of any human agency, to renew itself. It is this of which he speaks in "A Pippa Lilted": "It will be soon; / good things will happen." Or, the acceptance of the unheroic and unexalted in human nature, an honest perspective, allows "a pretty good world" in "Adults Only." Most important of all, however, and that which underlies Stafford's continued didacticism, is the faith that the life he once enjoyed upon the Kansas wilderness and the one he seeks to reclaim upon the modern wilderness is still dynamic and accessible.

Stafford seems to have been the first American poet to incorporate successfully the Emotive Imagination during the 1950s. Each succeeding volume by him has reconfirmed its viability and vitality to him as a poet. Yet, it is worth a final note to acknowledge again that he has never embraced this mode of poetry to the exclusion of other and more traditional kinds of verse.

The importance of the Emotive Imagination to these four poets and to others may rest on the premise that its use not be exclusive of other forms of poetry; it may be true that the method does not offer a sustaining idiom for a poet whose intent is experimentation over a continuing career. The achievements of Bly, Wright, Simpson, and Stafford nonetheless establish that its practice offers a major lyric experimentation in American poetry, one which lends itself abundantly to a variety of sensibilities and subjects, and one which has yielded individual poems of permanent importance to American letters.

Index